Hoi Toide on the Outer Banks

Walt Wolfram and Natalie Schilling-Estes

Hoi Toide on the Outer Banks

The

Story

of the

Ocracoke

Brogue

THE UNIVERSITY OF NORTH CAROLINA PRESS CHAPEL HILL & LONDON

© 1997 The University of North Carolina Press
All rights reserved
Manufactured in the United States of America

The paper in this book meets the guidelines
for permanence and durability of the Committee
on Production Guidelines for Book Longevity
of the Council on Library Resources.

Library of Congress
Cataloging-in-Publication Data
Wolfram, Walt, 1941–
Hoi toide on the Outer Banks:
the story of the Ocracoke brogue /
Walt Wolfram, Natalie Schilling-Estes.
p. cm.
Includes bibliographical references
and index.
ISBN 0-8078-2318-x (alk. paper). —
ISBN 0-8078-4626-0 (pbk.: alk. paper)
1. English language — Dialects — North
Carolina — Ocracoke Island.   2. Americanisms —
North Carolina — Ocracoke Island.   3. Popular
culture — North Carolina — Ocracoke Island.
4. Ocracoke Island (N.C.) — Social life and
customs.   I. Schilling-Estes, Natalie.   II. Title.
PE2927.O27W65   1997
427'.9756184 — dc20   96-32653
CIP

01 00 99 98 97   5 4 3 2 1

Contents

Illustrations

Maps

Tables

Preface

The first time we set foot on Ocracoke Island in the dead of winter 1992, we were followed there by a menacing nor'easter. We were torn: Should we leave the island quickly before the ferries stopped running and give up our opportunity to interview the respected O'cocker, Elizabeth Howard? Or should we stay and risk being marooned on the island? We chose to stay with Elizabeth Howard, listening while she told us stories about the way things were. Finally, she sent us on our way with a jar of fig preserves and a T-shirt reading, "Young'uns, hain't I been mommucked this day!!!" The weather certainly mommucked us that day as we attempted to leave the Outer Banks on highways flooded by the storm tide, but our positive impression of the people of Ocracoke was indelibly inscribed on that occasion. Our experience, combining risk from the elements with warm generosity from the people of Ocracoke, set the tone for the finest collaborative dialect study we have undertaken in all our years of language research.

This book is the manifestation of our study of the Ocracoke "brogue," which began in 1992 with our visit to Elizabeth Howard and continues to this day. Our goal is to describe the rich dialect heritage of the residents of Ocracoke, North Carolina, before the brogue vanishes. We attempt to describe the language in a way that is faithful to the detailed patterning of the dialect while making our account readable to the wide range of people who are interested in the speech of Ocracoke. Our first and foremost debt is to the islanders who generously tolerated our invasion of their island world in order to conduct the interviews that served as the primary source for our description. More than seventy longtime residents, ranging in age from ten to ninety-one, were interviewed and tape-recorded from 1992 through 1995, and we are deeply indebted to each person who so graciously responded to our sometimes intrusive probing of their everyday lives in search of dialect treasures. Everyone was extremely responsive, but a few people assumed key roles in offering continued assistance and suggestions. We kept coming back to Kenny Ballance, Dave Esham, Candy Gaskill, James Barrie Gaskill, Elizabeth Howard, Chester Lynn, and Rex O'Neal. Amazingly, they put up with us as, over and over, we asked "just one more dingbatter question." Sadly, we can no longer call on Elizabeth Howard, the first O'cocker we ever interviewed for this study and a source of great knowledge about island history and life. During the harsh winter of 1996, the island lost one of its great personal treasures, and we all lost a warm and generous friend. Unfortunately, several other O'cockers have also passed away since the inception of our study. We hope that our interviews with them will preserve some of the significant legacy of Ocracoke life and language.

There are a number of other O'cockers whom we wish to thank. One is Melinda Jackson, who has been incredibly patient and extremely helpful to the dingbatter linguists who crowd into the Pony Island Motel where she works. She is one of the few O'cockers who is strong enough to resist Walt's pleadings for an interview. We also deeply appreciate the cooperation of Larry Thompson, principal of the Ocracoke School, as well as Gail Hamilton, who volunteered her eighth grade class for an experimental curriculum on Ocracoke speech as a part of the study of North Carolina history. Thanks also to the Ocracoke Preservation Society, its past president, Kenny Ballance, and its current president, Ellen Fulcher Cloud, for support of this work as a preservation effort. We particularly appreciate Ellen Fulcher Cloud's extensive search of historical records on Ocracoke, which provided important historical background for our language study. Half the royalties from the sale of this book will be donated to the Ocracoke Preservation Society to further their important work. We hope that our commitment to documenting the brogue will underscore the seriousness of efforts to preserve dialects across America.

Interviews were conducted by members of the North Carolina Language and Life Project (NCLLP) and by students and staff at North Carolina State University. Walt and Marge Wolfram coordinated the efforts of the original fieldwork team; the fieldworkers were Paul Amash, Chris Craig, Kirk Hazen, Beth Renn, and Natalie Schilling-Estes. Thanks are due also to the fieldworkers in subsequent years who conducted more interviews and helped us fill some of the gaps in our study. Unfortunately, since this is an ongoing project with continuing student involvement, we cannot name all those who have received or have yet to receive their baptism in dialect study on Ocracoke.

A number of people were extremely helpful in the preparation of the book. Kirk Hazen has worked with the authors throughout this study and has assisted Walt Wolfram for several years in teaching the dialect curriculum in the Ocracoke School. Kathleen Hazen contributed cartographic and computer expertise and advice, and Keli Yerian helped configure some of the maps in addition to helping conduct interviews. Ann Ehringhaus lent her considerable photographic skill to the project by taking the photographs that accompany the text. Fellow linguists Barbara Fennell and Peter Trudgill were extremely patient and responsive to our questions about transcontinental connections for various dialect forms, and Carmine Prioli helpfully discussed broader-based cultural connections to other Outer Banks communities. Lucinda MacKethan introduced us to her close friends in the Ocracoke community, Dave and Jen Esham, and she also provided wise counsel at various points in the progression of this study. Wynne Dough, at the Outer Banks History Center, and Alton Ballance, local historian, schoolteacher, and author, were especially responsive to our inquiries about the history of the Outer Banks and Ocracoke. David Perry, Shelley Gruendler, and Pam Upton at the University of North Carolina Press efficiently guided the publication process and attended to the countless details that are inevitably associated with an undertaking of this scope. Jim Clark, director of the North Carolina State University Humanities Extension Program, offered expertise and wisdom, along with strong moral support, at strategic points as we put together our curriculum on the Ocracoke brogue.

Chris Estes gave generously of his time and expertise in making maps and editing the manuscript for readability. His support during the various phases of this project was indispensable, as was the support of Marge Wolfram, who was there from start to finish. She was especially good at being human when our focus on dialect structure became obsessive. Only Marge and Chris can really understand the sacrifices that spouses of compulsive and myopic researchers must endure. Thanks for your eternal patience.

We also gratefully acknowledge the funding for travel and research that we received from the William C. Friday Endowment Fund, the National Science Foundation (Grant SBR-93-19577), and the National Endowment for the Humanities (Grant RO-22749).

Hoi Toide on the Outer Banks

People come up to us, they think our accent's weird. But we think the same thing about them, you know. A lot of people, especially people from up North, they say, "Say something for us. Say *walk* or *water* or *hoi toide* or something like that."

Bubby Boos, age 18, 1993

I had a lady in here last week I had a battle with. You might as well say a battle with, because she came up to the counter, and she said "Speak!"
I said, "Excuse me?"
She said, "Speak!"
I was like, "Do I get a biscuit?"
She said, "I wanna hear you talk."

Candy Gaskill, age 28, 1995

I stand there, and they're watching me. They're watching me talk, and I feel conscious of it. . . . They'll get me to talk, and they'll ask me questions.

Elizabeth Parsons, age 59, 1993

The Roots of Ocracoke English

1

The Ocracoke dialect, or brogue, is one of the first things visitors to the island notice. This dialect is most distinctive for the way its speakers pronounce the *i* vowel as more of an *oy*, so that *high* and *tide* sound like *hoi* and *toide*. But a number of other traits also contribute to the "hoi toider" sound that is quite unlike the speech of the mainland southerners who are Ocracoke's neighbors. For example, Ocracokers give the *ow* sound in a word like *town* an unusual pronunciation that makes the word sound something like *tain*. They also pronounce their *r*'s more than do most mainlanders. Speakers from many parts of the eastern North Carolina mainland, especially older speakers, tend to pronounce words like *farm* and *cart* as *fahm* and *caht*, without the *r* sounds; Ocracokers, however, will most likely leave the *r*'s in. Ocracoke English is marked by some unusual grammatical variations, and visitors to the island might hear sentences such as "People *goes* to the store" instead of "People *go* to the store" or "It *weren't* me" instead of "It *wasn't* me." And what distinctive dialect would be complete without its share of unique words? Ocracokers are well known for their distinctive vocabulary, especially the word *mommuck*, which means 'to harass or bother', as in "Don't *mommuck* me; I've had a hard day." Other dialect words include *quamished*, which refers to having an upset stomach (as in "That ferry ride made me feel *quamished*"), and *call the mail over* for 'mail delivery to the island post office'. ("Is the mail *called over* yet? I'm expecting an important letter.")

People attempting to describe Ocracoke speech to outsiders often call it Shakespearean English, Elizabethan English, or Old English. The Ocracoke brogue also seems to remind some people of Irish or Scottish English, since speakers of those language varieties are said to speak a "brogue" as well. In fact, the word *brogue* comes from the Irish term *barroq*, which means 'to grab hold, especially with the tongue'.

On first consideration, Shakespearean English may seem like a good label for the Ocracoke brogue. After all, there were a number of explorations along the Virginia coast and North Carolina's Outer Banks in Shakespeare's day. And the first permanent English settlement in the New World was established in Jamestown, Virginia, in 1607, a full nine years before Shakespeare's death. So it is probable that the first settlers on the Outer Banks spoke a variety of English similar to that of Shakespeare, Sir Francis Bacon, Queen Elizabeth, and their contemporaries.

It is tempting to think that this older form of English might have been preserved on Ocracoke. After all, the island is separated from the mainland by twenty miles of water, well removed from the language evolution that occurred there over the centuries from Elizabethan times to the present day. A quick comparison of today's brogue with Shakespeare's writings reveals some interesting similarities that suggest Outer Banks English is indeed related to the English of almost four hundred years ago. For example, the word *mommuck* was widely used in sixteenth-century England, though its meaning was different back then (it actually meant 'to shred'). *Mommuck* even appears in one of Shakespeare's plays: "Hee did so set his teeth, and teare it. Oh, I warrant how he *mammockt* it" (*Coriolanus* I, iii, 71).

Is it possible, then, that Ocracoke English is really Elizabethan English, as some people claim? What a find that would be for scholars who study the histories of languages! Unfortunately, things aren't that simple. One fact about languages that all linguists agree on—and that many nonspecialists are well aware of—is that all languages, and all dialects, are constantly changing. If it weren't for the changing nature of language, varieties like Elizabethan English wouldn't have developed in the first place. The way Shakespeare talked or wrote would be the way we talk now. And anyone who has ever read one of his plays, or has even read something written in the 1800s, knows that such is not the case. In fact, the further back in time we go, the harder it becomes to understand texts written in what we think of as our own language. Thus, although it is possible to read and understand Shakespeare (at least with annotations), it's almost impossible for the nonexpert to pick up a work by Chaucer (who died in 1400) and be able to understand it unless it has been translated into modern English. And if we go even further back than that, English begins to look like a completely different language.

Languages change so drastically over time that linguists routinely separate a developing language into different stages or periods in order to analyze those changes. English is usually studied in terms of four significant historical periods. The first, Modern English, is the language we speak today. The second, Early Modern English (ca. 1500–1800), covers the Elizabethan period as well as the period of early exploration in the New World, including the first settlement on Ocracoke in 1715. The third, Middle English, is the variety spoken by Chaucer (ca. 1100–1500). And the fourth, the oldest form of the language, is Old English, which was spoken in England up until shortly after the Norman Invasion led by William the Conqueror.

To illustrate the point that languages change—sometimes radically—over time, here are four versions of the first verse of the Lord's Prayer, one from each period in the history of the English language:

Old English (about 950 A.D.):
Fader urer ðu bist in heofnas, sie gehalgad noma ðin

Middle English (about 1350 A.D.):
Oure fadir þat art in heuenes, halwid be þi name

Early Modern English (about 1550 A.D.):
O oure father which arte in heven, hallowed be thy name

Modern English (about 1985 A.D.):
Our father who is in heaven, may your named be sacred

The Old English version of more than a thousand years ago may not look much like English at all. But if you examine it closely, you can see the beginnings of a few Modern English words, such as *fader* for *father*, *urer* for *our*, and *noma* for *name*.

The tendency of languages to change over time has given rise to the different dialects of English that are familiar to us today. Speakers of a common language who become isolated from one another will gradually begin to speak different dialects of that language. Isolation can result from physical barriers such as mountains or water, or it can result from strong social or ethnic divisions. The essential quality of isolation, however, is that isolated people do not communicate or otherwise interact with other groups of people on a regular basis. Languages or dialects in secluded areas continue developing as time goes by, but development in different areas takes a unique course in each one, especially when contact between these areas is limited. Thus, Early Modern English split into American and British variants because the Atlantic Ocean lay between the colonists and their relatives at home. And the English that was originally brought to the New World already consisted of numerous dialects. The first settlers on Ocracoke most likely spoke a very different dialect from early colonists in Boston. Further, it is quite probable that even the small handful of people who settled the island came from a number of different areas themselves, each with its own dialect. All the disparate forms of speech brought to this country eventually evolved into the American English dialects we recognize today, such as southern, New England, and, of course, Outer Banks English.

Defining and naming the dialect areas of the United States is a complex matter, and dialectologists throughout the twentieth century have continued to propose various ways of dividing up the country's regional speeches. For our purposes in this book, we have adopted the relatively straightforward divisions for which most people already have an intuitive feel. When we refer to southern dialect areas, we mean those areas south of the Mason-Dixon line between Pennsylvania and Maryland. The South itself may be divided into several subregions, including Appalachian or highland southern and lowland southern (that is, the nonmountainous South). Within North Carolina, the lowland area encompasses the Coastal Plains region in the eastern portion of the state as well as the Piedmont region in the center of the state. Map 1 illustrates these dialect divisions.

It is important to remember that even when one group of speakers becomes totally isolated from other speakers, its language continues evolving, but in a different direction from everyone else's. Ocracoke might have been cut off from the mainland during its early history, but its language never became stagnant. Even if Shakespeare himself had built the first house in Ocracoke Village and then had traveled through time to visit the Outer Banks today, he would have a hard time understanding the language of his descendants on the islands, because the language he had originally brought to Ocracoke would have changed so much over the intervening centuries.

So, if Ocracoke English isn't an Elizabethan dialect that has been frozen in time since the seventeenth century, then what is it? On what dialects of Early Modern English is it based, and in what directions did it evolve from that point of origin? Is it kin to today's British or Australian English, as some tourists claim? Is it more like other American English dialects? Or is it unique, having evolved in ways that distinguish it from every other English dialect?

THE ORIGINS OF OCRACOKE ENGLISH

Beginning with their first explorations of the Outer Banks, British sea captains recognized that Ocracoke Inlet was a strategic passageway through the hazardous chain of barrier islands to mainland ports. Large ships could not pass through without assistance, however, so it was necessary to station pilots at the inlet to help guide the vessels. As more and more Europeans began inhabiting

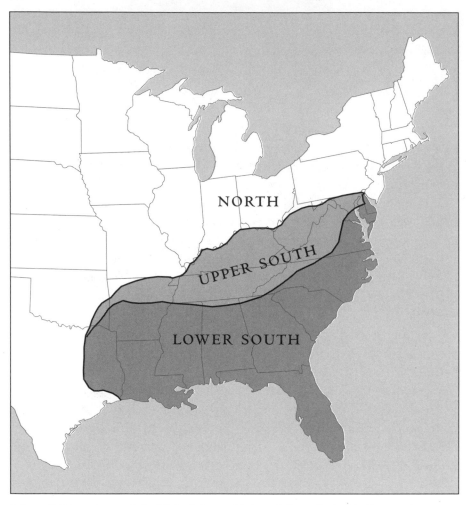

Map 1. Dialect Areas of the United States (Adapted from Craig M. Carver, *American Regional Dialects: A Word Geography* [Ann Arbor: University of Michigan Press, 1987], p. 247)

coastal Virginia and mainland North Carolina, ship traffic through Ocracoke Inlet increased to such a great extent that in 1715 the North Carolina Assembly passed what the old record books termed "An Act for Settling and Maintaining Pilots at Roanoke and Ocacock Inlett." Thus Pilot Town, later renamed Ocracoke Village, was born.

The first pilots who built temporary homes in the new village were most likely of English origin. By the time the community began to take on the character of a permanent settlement, around 1770 or so, most of the British from whom today's prominent island families are descended were already living on Ocracoke or in neighboring Portsmouth, across the inlet from Ocracoke Village. Many of these families had not immigrated directly from Britain but rather had lived for a while in the Virginia Tidewater area and the Albemarle Sound region of North Carolina. The surnames of these first inhabitants are still common on Ocracoke, including Bragg, Gaskins, Howard, Jackson, Stiron (today spelled Styron), and Williams. One well-known family, the O'Neals, are of Irish origin, as probably are the Scarboroughs, thought to be descended from Captain Edmund Scarborough, an Irishman who settled on the Eastern Shore of Virginia in the 1630s. Other Ocracoke families, such as the Austins, Ballances, and Midgetts, had established themselves on neighboring Banks islands before the turn of the nineteenth century.

What sort of English was spoken by early Ocracokers? We know for certain that it was some variety of Early Modern English, which, as mentioned above, is the name we give to the form of English spoken from some one hundred years before Shakespeare's day until about two hundred years after his death. Some characteristics of Early Modern English that distinguish it from today's Modern English include the use of several pronouns no longer common in our time, including *thou* for the singular *you*; different verb forms such as *sate* for the past tense of *sit* (as in "Yesterday she *sate* there"); *-eth* endings on certain verbs ("He *sitteth*"); the absence of the word *do* in places where we would use it today (as in, "Sits he in the chair?" and "Sit not there!"); and, certainly, many spelling differences that didn't affect how the language sounded but greatly affected how it looked on paper. Some remnants of Early Modern English that we do find in the Ocracoke brogue include the addition of *a-* (pronounced *uh*) before verbs

An aerial view of the lighthouse and Springer's Point.
(Photograph by Ann Sebrell Ehringhaus)

ending in -ing, as in "He went a-fishin'," as well as the use of distinctive words like *mommuck* and *quamished*.

One notable difference between the early English brought to Ocracoke and today's language was the pronunciation of certain vowels. For example, the *ay* sound in words such as *name* was pronounced like the vowel in Modern English *cat*, and the *i* sound in words such as *high* and *tide* sounded something like the vowel *uh* (as in *but*) followed quickly by *ee* (as in *beet*), resulting in *t-uh-ee-d*. This pronunciation is reminiscent of the *i* sound we hear on Ocracoke today, which many people think sounds like the *oy* in *boy* but which really falls somewhere in between the Early Modern English *i* sound and our *oy*.

Another Early Modern English vowel that sounds similar to the current pronunciation on Ocracoke is the *ow* vowel in a word like *house*, pronounced as *uh* (as in *but*) plus *oo* (as in *boot*), so that we get *h-uh-oo-s*. The *ow* sound on Ocracoke today is somewhat different from this earlier sound, since *house* comes out sounding something like *hice* rather than *h-uh-oo-s*. But both the *ow* and *i* sounds in current Ocracoke speech do come from their Early Modern English progenitors. Those same vowel sounds, which first came from England in the 1700s, developed along different lines in other American dialect areas. For example, in the mainland South *tide* is often pronounced as *tahd*, while in the North we find the long *i* of *tide*. On the other hand, in the Virginia Tidewater area, from which many of the Outer Banks's first families came, we can hear a pronunciation for words like *house* in which the *ow* sounds very much like the Ocracoke version of this vowel.

Although Ocracoke English is based on Early Modern English, we need to remember that there were many dialects of that early language, just as there are of its equivalent today. There is some question as to exactly which forms of Early Modern English played a role in shaping the early Ocracoke brogue. Much of the American South was settled by people from the south and west of England. But early settlers along the coastal areas of the South, including some Outer Banks families, may have come from England's eastern counties as well. We have found that today's Ocracoke brogue displays many features from southern and western England, along with a number from eastern England.

It is also likely that early Ocracoke speech was influenced by the Irish and Scots-Irish varieties of English. Many of the first Europeans to settle in southeastern North America were of Irish rather than English descent. In fact, by 1790 the Irish constituted fully one-eighth of the white population of the South. The Scots-Irish, who came from the province of Ulster in what is now Northern Ireland, were even more numerous. At the time of the American Revolution, there were already 250,000 Scots-Irish living in America; and from then until the end of the nineteenth century, they made up the largest single white ethnic group in the South. Although most of the Scots-Irish settled originally in Pennsylvania rather than the American South, many of these early immigrants and their descendants eventually made their way southward to the Carolinas.

The variety of Early Modern English spoken by the Scots-Irish of that period was probably as different from the English spoken in today's Great Britain as our modern American English is from British English. Interestingly, some of the major features that characterize dialects thought to derive from Scots-Irish are still found in Ocracoke English. One of these, shared by other dialects such as the Appalachian English spoken in the North Carolina mountains, is the use of *anymore* in affirmative sentences, as in "We watch a lot of videos *anymore*." Another prominent feature of Scots-Irish English is its formulation of sentences like "People *goes* to the mountains" or "Some of them *catches* fish" instead of "People *go* to the mountains" or "Some of them *catch* fish." Although we might think of *people goes* as being improper or "incorrect" English, dialect studies have shown that such constructions do not reflect lack of subject-verb agreement but rather a different agreement system. Certain nouns like *people* or *some* or *a few* are considered plural in standard English and therefore take verb forms that don't end in -*s*. But because these nouns do not themselves end in -*s*, the usual marker for plural nouns, many speakers of dialects that differ from the standard treat them like singular nouns. Even in varieties of English that are held in high regard by language purists, such as standard British English, we find rules for subject-verb agreement that differ from the American standard. Thus, while we Americans say "The government *was* debating the issue," the British can quite properly say "The government *were* debating the issue."

Ocracoke English, then, has its roots not in a single form of older English but in a number of Early Modern English dialects—dialects from Ireland, eastern England, and southwestern England. Map 2 shows where some of the most prominent features of the Ocracoke brogue most likely originated. The arrows indicate approximate migration routes. Note that, because so few settlers came directly from the British Isles to Ocracoke, our map follows the immigrants' travels to the major settlement areas of Jamestown and Philadelphia before they eventually made their way to Ocracoke.

We have already mentioned most of the language features listed on the map. These include pronunciations such as *hoi toide* for *high tide* and *park the car* rather than *pahk the cah*, as we might hear in the lowland South. We have also included some features related to sentence structure, such as the use of *anymore* in affirmative sentences to mean 'nowadays'; the use of *a-* before *-ing* verbs, as in "They were a-huntin'"; and the use of *weren't* for *wasn't*, as in "It weren't me." We haven't yet mentioned the pronunciation of *fish* as *feesh* or the use of double "helping verbs" like *might could*, as in "I *might could* do that." These latter two are general southern dialect features shared by Ocracokers. A final trait we have included is the pronunciation of *ain't* with an *h* in front of it. This characteristic is found in a number of isolated U.S. dialects, including Ocracoke English and Appalachian English, and represents an older pronunciation that has been preserved mainly in regions that historically have not had much contact with speakers of mainstream English.

Map 3 shows the major routes of Scots-Irish migration, which contributed to the close connections between the Outer Banks and Appalachian dialects today.

People sometimes think that because Ocracoke English sounds so different from surrounding dialects, it surely must have more exotic roots than a few older forms of British English—possibly Spanish, Italian, or even Arabic. In reality, although the early settlers on the Outer Banks included a few people who were not of English or Celtic origin, the only other ethnic group ever populous enough on the islands to have possibly influenced language development was that composed of people of African descent. There are only a couple of African Americans living on Ocracoke today, but at one point shortly before the Civil War, there were more than a hundred slaves on the island—almost one-fifth of the entire population of Ocracoke. Even in the earliest days of settlement, there were so many African American inhabitants that it appeared they might take over the piloting business from the English settlers who started it.

Although large numbers of African Americans once lived on Ocracoke, the Ocracoke brogue does not seem to have been influenced by a distinct African American dialect, or at least not by any dialect similar to the African American vernacular English we find in the mainland United States today. The one remaining African American Ocracoker with ancestral roots on the island has some Ocracoke English traits in her speech, but the dominant features are mostly those of African American vernacular English. White islanders, however, do not seem to use typical African American elements in their speech. For example, speakers of African American vernacular frequently drop the *-s* end-

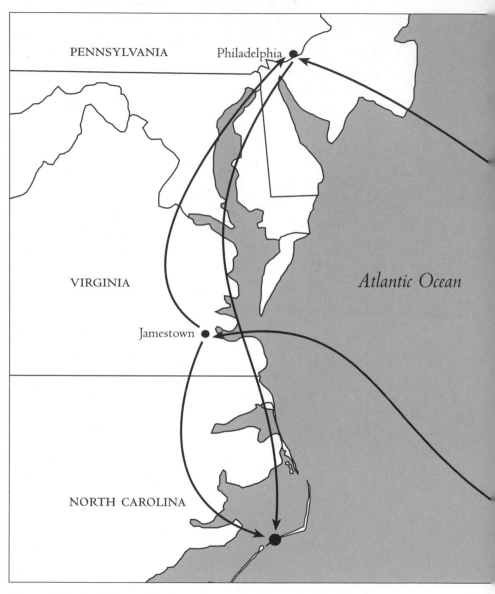

PENNSYLVANIA

Philadelphia

VIRGINIA

Atlantic Ocean

Jamestown

NORTH CAROLINA

Map 2. Historical Sources for Some Features of Ocracoke English
(Map drawn by Shelley Gruendler/Chris Estes)

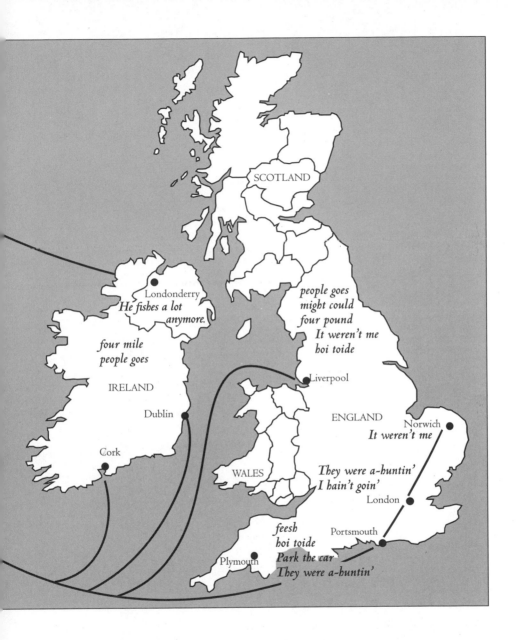

Londonderry
He fishes a lot anymore.

four mile
people goes

IRELAND

Dublin

Cork

SCOTLAND

people goes
might could
four pound
It weren't me
hoi toide

Liverpool

ENGLAND

Norwich
It weren't me

WALES

They were a-huntin'
I hain't goin'

London

feesh
hoi toide
Park the car
They were a-huntin'

Portsmouth

Plymouth

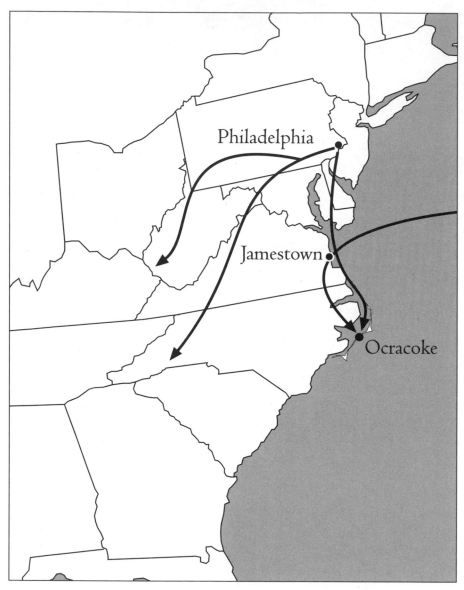

Map 3. Dialect Affinity between Ocracoke English and Appalachian English
(Map drawn by Shelley Gruendler/Chris Estes)

ings marking singular subject-verb agreement, as in "She go to the store." However, Ocracokers do use the -s, and not only in sentences that follow standard English patterns, such as "She goes to the store," but also in others where standard practice would drop the -s ("People goes to the store"). Other features associated with African American vernacular English—such as the absence of a form of *to be* in sentences like "She nice," or the use of *be* as in "Sometimes my ears be itching"—are not found in Ocracoke English either. So even though early Ocracokers had quite a bit of contact with African Americans, we have found no clear links between the brogue and the African American vernacular, which today is one of the most distinctive varieties of American English.

DEVELOPING AND MAINTAINING DISTINCT SPEECH

There is no question that the speech of Ocracoke is very different from that of mainland North Carolina. Mainlanders are quick to comment on the unusual sound of the "hoi toiders," saying that they can barely understand the brogue. In fact, a Raleigh-area television station once aired a story containing interviews with several "hoi toiders"—complete with subtitles so that off-islanders could understand what the Bankers were saying! Certainly, some of the language differences between Ocracokers and mainlanders stem from their different origins, which we have just discussed. But even if those origins had been exactly the same—even if the English, the Irish, and the Scots-Irish had distributed themselves evenly across the state when they immigrated to the New World—there would still be some compelling reasons for the sharp language differences we find today.

One key factor in the development of the unique Ocracoke brogue was the isolation of Ocracokers from the mainland, although in its earliest days Ocracoke Village was probably not as isolated as one might think. Rather, the village was a booming port town that enjoyed steady population growth up until the Civil War era. Census records tell us that the population of the island rose from 137 in 1800 to 536 in 1850. In fact, the Ocracoke-Portsmouth area was once the largest, busiest settlement in North Carolina. The shipping industry was largely responsible for Ocracoke's early success. At the height of Ocracoke

Inlet's popularity, island-based pilots guided as many as 1,400 ships a year through the narrow passageway to the mainland. Thanks to all this ship traffic, early residents of Ocracoke would have come into frequent contact with travelers from throughout England, the colonies, and the world.

A natural event altered all this. The other major passageway through the Outer Banks, Hatteras Inlet, located at the northern end of Ocracoke Island, had begun to close in the 1730s due to natural patterns of shifting sand common to all barrier islands. The shrinking inlet quickly became unsuitable for ship traffic, so ships were routed through Ocracoke Inlet, and the village there thrived. In 1846, however, a storm reopened Hatteras Inlet, and much traffic was diverted from Ocracoke. Also at this time, other means of transport, especially the railroad, began to grow in prominence, leaving Ocracokers cut off from the steady flow of travelers that had provided their contact with the outside world. Without such outside influence, the islanders' language began diverging from the language of other English-speaking people in the young United States.

The few records we have of Outer Banks speech in the mid-1800s suggest that the brogue had definitely taken on its distinctive character by this time. The memoirs of Alice Guthrie Smith, who was born in the late 1800s, include several dialect features that we find in today's brogue, including the use of *weren't* for *wasn't*, as in "He planted Irish potatoes, and there *weren't* no fertilizer then." (A portion of Smith's memoirs is reproduced in *Judgment Land: The Story of Salter Path*, book 1, by Kay Holt Roberts Stephens.) It is important to remember that although Ocracokers were isolated from much contact with the outside world after 1846, their language never stopped changing. It merely took a different course than dialects on the mainland.

Perhaps an influence on the developing speech of Ocracokers even greater than the natural events of 1846 were the manmade events of the 1860s—chiefly the Civil War. Outer Bankers were primarily pro-Union, probably because most of their trade routes ran up the coast to the north rather than westward to the southern mainland. In fact, the Outer Banks were occupied by Union troops for most of the war, beginning with the capture of Hatteras Inlet in 1861. Ocracokers' limited relations with mainland North Carolinians were virtually

Howard Street—a view of Ocracoke past. (Photograph by Ann Sebrell Ehringhaus)

terminated during the war; most interactions with outsiders on the isolated island were now with Northerners. It is likely that these communication patterns, as well as a strong desire on the part of Outer Bankers to separate themselves from the Confederates on the mainland, played a big part in shaping the brogue into a dialect that sounds different from the typical southern accent. Ocrakokers wishing to express their support for the Northern cause might even have attempted to sound more Northern and less Southern, whether consciously or unconsciously.

Using language to draw oneself closer to a particular group is by no means unique to the Ocracokers of the 1860s. Speakers of all dialects and all languages tend to alter their speech patterns to indicate social alliances that are important to them. And most of us have probably noticed that when we wish to identify with a certain group, we may speak a little more like people in that group than we normally would. The same thing might have happened with Ocracokers during the Civil War. They wanted to fit in with the North—not the South—so they didn't want to talk like lowland southerners. Even today, certain features in their speech sound quite northern. For example, the pronunciation of the *r* sound, mentioned earlier, is very different from the traditional "*r*-less" speech of the lowland South. Ocracokers also tend to pronounce their *aw* sounds, as in *caught* and *bought*, in a more northern than southern way. In fact, sometimes when they say these words they sound more like New Yorkers than North Carolinians.

After the Civil War, the importance of both Ocracoke and Hatteras Inlets declined drastically, chiefly due to improved means of land transportation and inland canals, which allowed more goods to be shipped through the ports of Norfolk and Morehead City. The population of Ocracoke Village leveled off and then began declining; and even Hatteras, which had passed Ocracoke in importance just before the war, saw its last commercial ship in 1895. The Outer Bankers thus became more isolated than ever before, and their language was allowed to develop in its own way.

But despite their decreasing commercial importance, the Outer Banks islands were never completely cut off from outside contact. Fishing and other maritime enterprises necessitated continued association with coastal cultures to the north, including the people of the Chesapeake Bay area, whose dialect today bears many resemblances to the brogue. Even people from the mainland South contributed to the Outer Banks economy in their own way. Almost since the Outer Banks region was first settled, mainlanders from North Carolina and other states had enjoyed summer vacations on the unspoiled beaches. There are reports of tourists' visiting Ocracoke and Portsmouth for sea bathing as early as the 1750s and 1760s; one Outer Banks town, Nags Head, was specifically designed with tourists in mind. In fact, Nags Head was a well-known resort as early as the 1830s. It is not likely, however, that tourists from mainland North

Carolina had much effect on the development of the Outer Banks brogue. Travelers to the Banks in the 1800s tended to comment on how the island residents kept to themselves rather than socializing with tourists—possibly because the Bankers were too busy trying to scratch an uncertain living from the islands to spend time with wealthy plantation owners from the rich farmland to the west.

Certainly, making ends meet on the Outer Banks has never been easy. Even in its early days as a thriving port town, Ocracoke Village could support only so many pilots. The rest of the populace had to support itself by other means, whether by ship-related trades such as boat building and repair or by raising livestock, fishing, and hunting wildfowl. Growing crops on a large scale was impossible on these small islands, so Bankers had little in common with farmers on the neighboring mainland.

Other money-making activities before the turn of the twentieth century were built around the danger the islands posed to passing ships. In its early history the seas off the Outer Banks were famous for the numerous shipwrecks that occurred there, earning the area the nickname of the Graveyard of the Atlantic. Some Ocracokers served as lifeguards, operating lifesaving stations built at either end of the island in the latter half of the nineteenth century by the U.S. Lifesaving Service (which later was merged with the Revenue Cutter Service and was renamed the U.S. Coast Guard). A handful of islanders also served as lighthouse keepers, some working at the Shell Castle Lighthouse, completed in 1798 and located just inside the entrance to Ocracoke Inlet, and others at the Ocracoke Lighthouse, which was built in 1823 and still stands today.

Islanders sometimes attempted to augment their incomes by "wrecking"—that is, salvaging usable and saleable items from ships that had wrecked on their beaches—but such an occupation certainly provided no one with a steady source of money. There are numerous romantic tales of thriving pirate communities on the Outer Banks, but in reality such stories are highly exaggerated. Historical records indicate that the infamous Edward Teach, known as Blackbeard, really did live on Ocracoke for a brief time and was even killed there in the Battle of Ocracoke Inlet in 1718. However, the so-called Golden Age of pirating on the Outer Banks lasted for only about five years (1713–18), and only a few acts of piracy actually took place along the Banks.

Although outsiders often think that Ocracokers primarily make their living by fishing and have done so throughout their history, it was not until 1931 that a fishing industry of any size was able to develop on the island, thanks to the dredging out of Cockle Creek and the construction of Silver Lake Harbor, two developments that made it possible for larger ships to anchor in Ocracoke Village. Similarly, improved transportation and refrigeration methods were needed before significant quantities of the daily catch could be transported to the mainland for sale without heavy spoilage. Even with such advances in the fishing industry in the first half of the twentieth century, Ocracokers did not achieve prosperity. Islanders struggled to compete with the immense seafood industry centered in the Chesapeake Bay to the north; in addition, the Great Depression hit the islands with a vengeance. Jobs became so scarce that many families moved away from Ocracoke to find work in such northern ports as Wilmington, Delaware, and Philadelphia, Pennsylvania. Often these families returned to Ocracoke after years or even decades, bringing with them new dialect influences from these northern cities.

One language feature that links Ocracoke with northern areas like Philadelphia, as well as with highland areas such as Appalachia, is the use of positive *anymore*, which we have already mentioned several times. In many dialects, including lowland southern varieties, *anymore* is not used in positive sentences like "She sells a lot of fish anymore," even though it freely occurs in corresponding negative sentences: "She doesn't sell much fish anymore." (Of course, *anymore* is widespread in nonnegative questions and conditionals, as in "Does she live there anymore?" and "If you come here anymore, I'll call the police.") Because they do not typically use positive *anymore*, lowland southerners have a hard time figuring out what it means. Ocracokers and other Outer Bankers, by contrast, use the expression on a daily basis.

The fortunes of Ocracoke improved during World War II, when several military bases were established on the island. However, it was not until after the war that new jobs really opened up on the island in significant numbers. The tourism industry, long a small segment of the Ocracoke economy, blossomed in the postwar years—especially after 1953, when all of Ocracoke Island, except for Ocracoke Village and the immediate vicinity, was designated as national park-

Rex O'Neal tending his pound nets in the sound. (Photograph by Herman Lankford)

land. Although the annexation of Ocracoke to the Cape Hatteras National Seashore meant that some islanders were forced to sell their lands to the federal government and that no one could build on most of the island's 30,000-plus acres, most residents eventually recognized the benefits this action brought to their island. Ocracoke was saved from the blight of uncontrolled growth, especially the tourist-related development that marred the seascape and wreaked havoc on the natural ecology in such places as Nags Head to the north and Myrtle Beach to the south. In addition, the National Park Service and the state-owned ferry service, set up to bring tourists to the island, offered new jobs to residents.

Another key event in bringing tourism-related jobs to the island and luring former residents back from the northern cities was the completion in 1957 of a hard-surface highway reaching from the village to near Hatteras Inlet. Regular ferry routes from the village to the mainland and from Hatteras Island to Ocracoke were also established at about the same time, and tourists now flock to the more accessible island in ever-increasing numbers.

O'Neal's dock at "the Creek." (Photograph by Ann Sebrell Ehringhaus)

THE EFFECT OF TOURISM ON THE OCRACOKE BROGUE

How has the growing tourist industry of the past thirty or so years affected the Ocracoke brogue? Or the fact that in recent years, outsiders have begun moving to Ocracoke to live? Many old island families complain that the brogue is being lost and that their children now speak just like everyone else, thanks to their frequent contact with off-islanders.

To get an idea of how the brogue has been changing over time, we compared the speech patterns of older, middle-aged, and younger Ocracokers. Not surprisingly, we found that many older Ocracokers seem to speak in a stronger brogue than their younger neighbors, one full of older language traits not typically used by younger islanders, such as *hain't* for *ain't*, *hit* for *it*, and the *a-* prefix with *-ing* verbs ("Wallace was a-fishin'").

We were surprised to find, however, that the speakers who actually sound the most "brogue-ish" of all are not necessarily the very oldest islanders, but rather the middle-aged men, especially one core group of close friends who work and socialize together on a daily basis. This close-knit group displays many of the speech traits that we have already introduced as characteristic of the brogue and will describe more thoroughly in the following chapters. Why would middle-aged men have a thicker brogue than older islanders? If the brogue were really dying out, as some islanders claim, we would expect speakers in their forties and fifties to sound less like "hoi toiders" than their older neighbors. Could it be that the islanders are mistaken, and the dialect they think is weakening is actually getting stronger? Not really. It turns out that Ocracokers, who have long maintained a deep interest in their own speech patterns, show a keen intuition about their language and how it relates to their identity.

The youngest Ocracokers do, in general, sound much less broguelike than older island residents. For example, we don't hear much of the traditional *hoi toide* vowel sound in the speech of people twenty-five and younger. At the same time some brogue features are dying out, though, young islanders are actually *increasing* their use of a couple of features associated with the traditional dialect. For example, some of the same young people who have almost eliminated the *hoi toide* vowel in their speech will use typical island sentence structures, such as "It weren't me," more than older speakers. And like their older relatives, young Ocracokers don't always substitute southern pronunciation features for features of the traditional brogue. Instead, they tend to adopt more northern-sounding traits—especially in areas having strong associations with island life. For example, although we may hear a few southern-sounding pronunciations like *tahm* for *time* or *own* for *on* among young islanders, we would rarely ever hear *hah tahd* for the well-known Ocracoke phrase *hoi toide*. Instead, we'd be likely to hear the northern *high tide*.

This adoption of northern as well as southern dialect traits is due in part to the fact that there are quite a few nonsoutherners among the tourists who visit and the new residents who move to Ocracoke. We might be tempted to think that another strong factor contributing to the rise in northern speech patterns on Ocracoke is the arrival of television—particularly cable TV. In fact, older Ocracokers often complain that TV is eroding the brogue quicker than tourism ever could. However, linguists who study dialects have shown, time and time again, that TV and other mass media have very little effect on people's speech patterns, despite the fact that the media exposes us to accents from across the country—particularly the ultra-standard-sounding English of news reporters and other authoritative commentators. The reason why TV has so little effect on the way we speak is that people's speech is most influenced by those with whom they come into daily, face-to-face contact. Distant actors and anchors simply don't stand a chance when they come up against the local speech patterns we're exposed to every day.

Another reason young Ocracokers are opting to sound northern rather than southern as they come into more contact with the outside world is that they want to ensure that their speech remains distinct from that of the neighboring mainland. Islanders of all ages are proud of their heritage, and even the youngest ones still want to be identified as Ocracokers, even though their decreasing isolation—and the passage of time itself—is causing the traditional brogue to fade away.

But if the brogue really is dying out over time, why don't the oldest islanders have a stronger brogue than the group of middle-aged men we mentioned above? One possible explanation is that these middle-aged men are exaggerating their island dialect, consciously or not, because they want there to be no mistake that they are "real" Ocracokers and not tourists or new residents recently relocated from the mainland. After all, islanders in this age group are those who grew up in the 1950s and 1960s, when tourism first became a major force on the island. And although tourism brought a needed boost to the Ocracoke economy, the sudden influx of outsiders into the secluded village was seen as a threat as well as a blessing. What would happen to traditional, quiet island ways when big-city tourists began insisting on all the modern conveniences, including upscale hotels and fast-food restaurants? Worse yet, what about all the new permanent residences for outsiders being constructed on lands once belonging to

Ocracoke's oldest families? Although they could do little to stem the tide of development on the island, Ocracokers who are now in their middle years could resist the encroachment of the mainland dialect by making their own dialect stronger. And that seems to be exactly what they did, or at least what one small, close-knit group of men did.

Middle-aged women on Ocracoke don't seem to place as much social value on a strong dialect as do men. This is not at all unusual: in communities throughout the Western world that linguists have studied, we have found that women typically speak a more standard form of their language than men. The reasons for this gender differentiation are by no means certain. One possibility on Ocracoke is that women usually hold jobs that bring them into more frequent contact with outsiders than men; often, the women run tourist shops and work as store cashiers, while the men go fishing and crabbing with fellow islanders. Just because women use more standard speech, though, doesn't mean that they never use the brogue. Many still use a version of the traditional dialect, particularly when talking among themselves. Unlike some men, who are ready to "put on the brogue" for outsiders, women are more prone to keep it to themselves and to use it mainly for their own purposes.

We should also keep in mind that there are a number of middle-aged and older islanders, male and female, who don't speak with a strong brogue simply because their families historically spoke a more "standard" English than other Ocracoke families, perhaps because they spent a lot of time off the island or because they came into frequent contact with outsiders who visited the island. Another reason why certain Ocracokers might choose to speak with less of a brogue than others is that "nonstandard" English is often looked down upon by those who pride themselves on their "correct" speech. In this book, we hope to argue convincingly that dialects like the Ocracoke brogue should not be condemned just because they're not considered standard. We hope to show that all language varieties, whether or not they appear in textbooks or are taught in the classroom, are characterized by regularly patterned features. These patterns exist in speakers' unconscious minds and are organized according to strict, though unspoken, rules, just as the variety of English we learn in school is governed by certain set rules. And even if certain dialect rules are different from the rules in grammar books, they are not random or sloppy or haphazard. They are merely different.

For example, we might think that the sentence "It weren't me" reflects ignorance on the part of the speaker, who doesn't realize that the "correct" form of the verb should be *wasn't*. However, if we closely study the use of *was* and *were* in Ocracoke speech, we find that Ocracokers are not using *weren't* randomly or incorrectly. Rather, they have an unconscious rule in mind that tells them to use the *were* form any time they utter a negative sentence but to stick with *was* in the affirmative. Thus, the same Ocracokers who say *it weren't* and *she weren't* will also say *it was, she was*, and perhaps even *they was*. The way Ocracokers use *was* and *were* certainly does not conform to standard English rules. But Ocracokers do have a rule, and they follow it as faithfully as people who strive for standard speech stick by their own *was/were* rule.

Similarly, when we encounter an *a-* in front of *-ing* verbs, as in "He went a-hunting," we might think that the speakers simply add the *a-* to every *-ing* word or that they randomly use the *a-* when they want to sound especially "quaint" — perhaps when they're telling a story about an event that happened in a small town years ago. However, when we really study this feature, we find that there is a whole set of rules telling speakers when to use the *a-* prefix and when not to. For example, the *a-* is only used with *-ing* words that act as verbs, as in "She went a-fishing," but not with *-ing* words that act as nouns, as in "He likes a-dancing."

If nonstandard dialects have such strict rules, why are they considered to be uneducated, ungrammatical, and socially unacceptable? The reasons are purely social and have nothing to do with the underlying structure of the dialects themselves. Linguistically, all languages and dialects are equally systematic — and equally suitable for the expression of even the most complex notions. On this level, socially stigmatized dialects are just as grammatical as their more socially acceptable counterparts. Dialects take on heightened social standing when they are spoken by socially favored people, not because they're linguistically "better" than other dialects. In fact, the same dialect trait may fall in and out of favor during the course of a language's evolution — or may even be considered proper in one dialect but improper in another. We have already mentioned that "the government *are*" is quite proper in standard British English, even though it just sounds wrong to American ears.

Whatever the reasons behind people's scorn for different dialects, the result is a strong pressure for brogue speakers to stifle their dialect. And even though a small group of middle-aged Ocracokers has managed to briefly revive the brogue among themselves, the speech patterns of younger residents reveal that the brogue in its traditional form is weakening as time goes by. In fact, the brogue is fading at such an alarming rate that it is now known as an *endangered dialect*, a term we discuss further in Chapter 6. (We have also put off our discussion of the possibility of "rescuing" the dying brogue until that chapter.) For now, we invite you to explore in more detail the vocabulary, pronunciation traits, and sentence structures that make the brogue special. In the process, we hope you develop the same appreciation we feel for the brogue and for all dialects, standard-sounding or not, that combine to make English the rich language it is today.

THE DISTRIBUTION OF BROGUE FEATURES

As we explore some of the features of the Ocracoke brogue, it is important to keep two points in mind. First, many of the features we describe for Ocracoke are not unique to this island specifically or even to the Outer Banks in general, but are found in other regions of the United States as well. Interestingly, one of the regions whose dialect most resembles the brogue is Appalachia. In many respects, the speech of Ocracoke is more like speech in the mountains of western North Carolina than that of the intervening lowland areas. In part, the similarity is due to a common Scots-Irish ancestry, although the Scots-Irish influence is certainly stronger in Appalachia than on Ocracoke. The other reason for the shared language features is no doubt the speakers' historical isolation from surrounding mainland areas. Many parts of Appalachia, far distant from regular transportation and communication routes because of the difficult mountainous terrain, existed in a kind of isolation similar to that created by the stretch of water that separates the Outer Banks from the mainland.

Second, we must remember that the speech characteristics we describe are not necessarily used by all Ocrakers. Although speakers do not select dialect features at random, it is sometimes difficult to predict exactly which structures will wind up together in one person's speech. This is particularly true for middle-aged and younger speakers, who use certain traditional features in their speech while relinquishing others. For example, younger speakers may continue using *weren't* in "She weren't there" but drop the traditional *hoi toide* vowel pronunciation. Or they may still say *quamish*, as in "*quamished* in the stomach," while no longer using *meehonkey* to refer to the island version of hide-and-seek.

So what makes the Ocracoke dialect unique? It is not the few language features that we have found only in the Outer Banks region, or the even fewer features we have found only on Ocracoke, but the particular way in which those features are combined that sets this dialect apart from other American English dialects. In this respect, the brogue is similar to a new recipe that has been created by mixing some well-known ingredients with a few lesser-known ingredients in an imaginative way. The resultant dish tastes quite unlike any previous one, but the uniqueness is found mostly in the mix, not in the individual components. We'll begin to get a taste for the unique mix that constitutes Ocracoke speech as we look at particular language structures and show how they are similar to and different from those of other dialects of American English.

What's in an O'cocker Word?

2

On the first night of our first big research trip to Ocracoke, several of us were invited to have dessert at the house of a well-known island family. When we arrived, we were surprised to discover that the women who had invited us had not told their husbands we would be coming; they had assumed, quite correctly, that the men would be suspicious of outsiders who traveled to a remote island to conduct some sort of scientific study of people's speech. During the course of the evening, we naturally began talking about the Ocracoke brogue. One of the older gentlemen in the family, Wallace Spencer, suddenly turned to the youngest fieldworker in our group, whose name was Chris, and said, "I bet you never heard the word *meehonkey* before. I bet you can't find out what it means." Wallace kept teasing Chris until finally, at the end of the evening, he relented and explained that *meehonkey* refers to a game of hide-and-seek that islanders used to play some decades ago.

A day or so later, Wallace Spencer invited Chris to his house, where he cooked dinner for him, presented him with a gift of fresh seafood, and, at long last, even agreed to be tape-recorded so we could include his speech in our study.

This story illustrates the symbolic role that dialect vocabulary may play in identifying people either as part of a social group or as outsiders who don't really fit in. By telling his young visitor about an island word that few outsiders had ever heard before, Wallace Spencer demonstrated his willingness to accept Chris—if not the other fieldworkers—into his community. Now, our research team has been so graciously accepted into Ocracoke social circles that a couple of diehard islanders actually use traditional island terms like *wampus cat* to address the team leader, Walt Wolfram.

Because their vocabulary is so much a part of how Ocracokers define themselves—and because unusual dialect words are so much fun—we begin our detailed description of the features of the Ocracoke brogue with a discussion of vocabulary. Following this discussion is a list of some of the vocabulary words that characterize the Ocracoke dialect. Our list is necessarily limited, because every dialect is composed of thousands and thousands of vocabulary words, some of which are unique to one dialect and others of which are shared with neighboring or otherwise similar varieties.

DEFINING THE DIALECT WORD

At first glance, the meanings of some of the dialect words presented here may seem fairly obvious, but as we look more closely, we will see that the precise meanings of these words can be difficult to pin down. There are several reasons for this difficulty. First, the relationship between a word and the object or idea it denotes is arbitrary—that is, there is no one "true" name for an object. For example, we call a swimming creature with fins and a tail *a fish* in English, *un pez* in Spanish, and *un poisson* in French. Even among dialects of the same language, we find different words for the same objects or ideas. In Raleigh, North Carolina, for example, we might say to someone who won't leave us alone, "Don't bother me," while on Ocracoke we'd say, "Don't mommuck me!" Thus it is

Walt Wolfram and Natalie Schilling-Estes interview David Esham on his boat. (Photograph by Herman Lankford)

hard to tell exactly what a given term might mean in a particular dialect, even if we're sure we know what it means in our own language variety.

Another reason for the trouble we have in coming up with exact definitions for dialect words is that most words do not have one precise meaning, but rather several slightly disparate meanings that are not always differentiated clearly from one another. Often, one dialect will adopt one of these submeanings as the primary meaning of a word while another dialect will choose an alternate submeaning. For example, on Ocracoke the word *mommuck*, which historically meant 'to tear or to shred', has taken on the primary meaning 'to bother or mess with a person'. But in the mainland area of Robeson County, North Carolina, which is separated from Ocracoke by a couple of hundred miles, *mommuck* means 'to make a mess of', as in "Don't you *mommuck* up your homework!" Speakers of these two dialects have adjusted the original meaning of one term in related but distinct ways. Of course, in most American English dialects, *mommuck* has vanished completely.

Quite naturally, the meanings of words change over the course of time. The range of meanings a word covers may expand, so that a word like *frigidaire*, which originally was the name of one particular brand of refrigerator, has come to be used for all types of refrigerators, on Ocracoke as in a number of regions in the South. This broadening of the meanings of specific brand names is fairly common in all American English dialects. Across the country, people use words like *kleenex* to mean 'tissue', *Coca-Cola* to refer to any cola drink, and *xerox* to refer to all photocopiers, regardless of brand, as well as to the actual act of making copies on these machines.

Similarly, on Ocracoke and in other coastal dialect areas, words that started out as nautical terms have now taken on other meanings. For example, *scuttle*, which originally referred to a small hatch in a boat or ship, is now used on Ocracoke to refer to a small space in a house as well. And *scud*, originally a nautical term meaning 'to run in front of a gale with little or no sail set', is now used to refer to automobile trips, so that an islander may "take a scud around the island." In fact, on Ocracoke *scud* is now used in this new sense far more often than it is used with reference to boats.

Words can also narrow in scope, so that terms like *creek* or *ditch*, originally meaning any small body of water (still the meaning in most dialects), today can be used to refer to specific places on Ocracoke Island: Silver Lake harbor is known simply as *the Creek*, and the mouth of this harbor is called *the Ditch*. This constriction in meaning of general terms for geographic features to names for specific locations seems to be common on Ocracoke, especially when the word *down* appears in front of the place name, as in *down Creek*, which refers to the main part of the village by Silver Lake, and *down Base*, which refers to the Coast Guard base. Because Ocracokers traditionally have based their economy on their natural surroundings, they are so thoroughly familiar with the island that they can identify every one of its features by a specific name. On Map 4, a number of Ocracoke locations are identified by their local names. Some of these names are general geographic terms that have been narrowed in meaning to refer to one specific locale; others are simply traditional Ocracoke place names.

Besides broadening or narrowing in meaning, words can also acquire more positive or negative connotations than they originally had. For example, *offshore*, which originally simply meant 'located off the coast', is now used negatively— if good-naturedly—to refer to a person who is outlandish or crazy: "That Kenny is so *offshore* he can't get back in!" Interestingly, *offshore* is somewhat akin in its development to *outlandish* on the mainland. At one point, *outland* referred to an outlying geographical location, but over time its meaning was extended to encompass personality, so that an outlandish person is someone who acts strange or odd. Similarly, in Ocracoke speech, terms for people from nearby island and coastal areas, such as *Hatterasser* (a person from Hatteras) and *Kinnykeeter* (someone from Kinnakeet) may be used to suggest that the people being discussed aren't as smart or as respectable as they could be. On the other side of the coin, *O'cocker* (pronounced *OH-cock-er*), a shortened form of *Ocracoker*, generally carries positive associations related to being an accepted member of the Ocracoke community. It is common for residents of a particular area to use shortened versions of the place name when making fond reference to their community (for example, *Philly* for *Philadelphia*).

The use of *offshore* to mean 'outlandish' also illustrates another way the meanings of words can change over time, as words that originally denoted an object or a location in the physical world come to refer to a mental state or other abstract notion. *Mommuck*, which used to mean the tearing or shredding of some object, now has more to do with a sort of shredded state of mind. "Young'uns, hain't I been mommucked this day!" certainly doesn't mean "Haven't I literally been torn to pieces!" Such nonliteral use of words, or *metaphor*, is a common way in which languages extend word meanings.

Words and their various meanings can be added to or lost from the vocabulary of a dialect area. Sometimes a word disappears because the people who used it no longer need to talk about the thing the word stood for. On Ocracoke the word *meehonkey*, which refers to an islandwide game of hide-and-seek, is

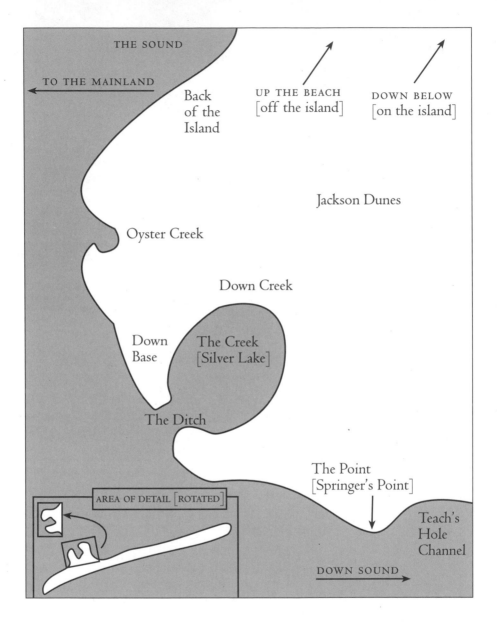

THE SOUND

TO THE MAINLAND

Back
of the
Island

UP THE BEACH
[off the island]

DOWN BELOW
[on the island]

Jackson Dunes

Oyster Creek

Down Creek

Down
Base

The Creek
[Silver Lake]

The Ditch

The Point
[Springer's Point]

Teach's
Hole
Channel

AREA OF DETAIL [ROTATED]

DOWN SOUND

Map 4. Ocracoke Place Names (Map drawn by Shelley Gruendler/Chris Estes)

rapidly fading from use, because children no longer play this large-scale version of the game. It is interesting to note, however, that some expressions have been retained even though their original meanings no longer apply. Ocracokers still ask one another, "Is the mail called over yet?" when they want to know if the mail has been delivered, even though this phrase refers to something they haven't done on Ocracoke for decades: calling out the names of those who had received mail when the mail boat arrived from the mainland.

When new objects or ideas are introduced into a dialect area, it makes sense that new words would be added to the vocabulary to describe these novelties. Sometimes these words are made up, as with *whoop and holler* (another word for a hide-and-seek game), and sometimes they're borrowed from another dialect or even another language. For example, *pizer* (pronounced pie-zer) was originally borrowed from the Italian *piazza* 'porch', an architectural feature much more common in warm Mediterranean countries like Italy than in the damp, rainy British Isles from which most of Ocracoke's early settlers came.

New words can also supplant older terms, forcing the old words to take on different meanings or pushing them out of the language completely. *Foreigner*, the traditional term for 'outsider' or 'someone from off-island', has been replaced in Ocracoke speech by *dingbatter*, a term that apparently is derived from the 1970s sitcom *All in the Family*. In this show, still seen in reruns, Archie Bunker regularly refers to his wife Edith as a "dingbat" when she displays a lack of common sense. The reason the term seems to be such a fitting replacement for *foreigner* is that, as used on TV, it not only literally referred to a person on the show but also strongly implied that this character was gullible and naive. Ocracokers took those implications of the word *dingbat* and applied them to their term *dingbatter*. They now have a single word that conveys many of their feelings toward visitors who come to the island and get into ridiculous situations because they're unfamiliar with island life. Interestingly, this word, which once meant 'a silly or naive person' and now means 'outsider' on Ocracoke, originally carried other meanings that have little or nothing to do with the word's current usage. At one point, *dingbat* meant something like 'thingamajig'—that is, some sort of unspecified object. Another of its older meanings was 'an object thrown at people'.

Walt Wolfram and Natalie Schilling-Estes chat casually with Chester Lynn. (Photograph by Herman Lankford)

Even linguists get new words from other dialects and sometimes change the meanings to suit their needs. Since we started studying the Ocracoke brogue, we've adopted the word *mommucked* into our own speech. Now we can't imagine how else to describe how we sometimes feel at the end of a long day in the office. We've even borrowed a word Ocracokers don't use much anymore, *meehonkey*, although we've changed its meaning quite a bit. We use it as a silly nickname (as in "Hey, Meehonkey, where are you going?") or as an adjective that ranges in meaning from 'silly' or 'stupid' to 'shallow' (as in "I wanted to do well on that paper I wrote, but I did a meehonkey job"). The bizarre series of meaning changes this word has undergone since it first crept into the Ocracoke vocabulary (most likely as an imitation of a goose call) serves as a good, if rather outlandish, illustration of how difficult it really can be to determine the meanings of dialect words with any certainty. *Meehonkey* also shows us that it's no easy task to trace meaning changes through time and across dialect areas, because these changes may be quite unpredictable, and in some cases, even creatively bizarre.

THE RANGE OF DIALECT WORDS

Apart from the difficulties of pinpointing the meanings of Ocracoke words, we also faced the problem of choosing just which words we should include in our vocabulary list. If we limited ourselves to words used exclusively on the island, we wouldn't be presenting a complete picture of the vocabulary that characterizes the Ocracoke brogue. This vocabulary consists not only of words that are found only on Ocracoke, such as *meehonkey*, but also of general Outer Banks terms like *mommuck*, general southern expressions like *fixin' to*, and northern words like *comforter*.

In addition, not all Ocracokers use or are even familiar with all the terms that we consider part of the Ocracoke vocabulary. Whereas just about everybody seems to use *mommuck*—and the word even appears on souvenir T-shirts sold to dingbatters—it seems that only older Ocracokers use the term *meehonkey* in natural conversation. Middle-aged islanders are familiar with the word, but we often have to prompt them to get them to remember that some of their older relatives used to play this game. And when we asked students at Ocracoke School about the term, they looked at us like we were offshore. Not only did these young islanders not use the word *meehonkey* or play the game, they hadn't even heard of it before—at least not until a couple of the students went home and asked their parents and grandparents about it. Similarly, the youngest Ocracokers regularly use some words, like *dingbatter*, that older people may know only vaguely or not at all. When the meanings of words alter over time, the confusion mounts. Old Ocracokers use the word *foreigner* to refer to tourists from off-island. When young people hear this term, however, they probably think only of someone from France or Germany or the like, because they now call outsiders by the newer name of *dingbatters*.

The waters get even muddier when we consider that there are certain Outer Banks and general southern terms that Ocracokers are familiar with but don't use, along with others that they don't know at all. For example, a number of Ocracokers are well acquainted with the Harkers Island term for outsiders, *dit-dots*, though they never use the word themselves. Conversely, Ocracokers do use some words known but not employed by other Outer Bankers or mainland southerners, in addition to words that we hear frequently in these other dialect areas.

Ultimately, we have to decide where to draw the line when it comes to the special vocabulary of a dialect. Sometimes what seems like a dialect word is really a relatively common word that is simply pronounced differently or used in an atypical way in a sentence. In the list below we have, for the most part, excluded words that simply represent dialect pronunciations (for example, *extry* for 'extra' or *feller* for 'fellow') as well as expressions that represent dialect sentence structures (for example, "We're in for some weather"). However, we have included a few exceptions where a pronunciation difference has resulted in the creation of a new word (as in *Co-cola* for 'Coca-Cola' or *skeeters* for 'mosquitoes') or common words are used in an idiomatic sentence structure (as in "call the mail over").

In this respect, our inventory differs from popular accounts of regional speech that tend to mix genuinely unique vocabulary words with unusual pronunciations and proverbial sayings. We have here restricted ourselves to the presentation of a dialect vocabulary, leaving discussions of pronunciation and grammar to subsequent chapters and the compilation of "sayings" to a future work. For reasons discussed above, though, we have not limited ourselves to words found exclusively on Ocracoke or other Outer Banks islands. We have also included a smattering of the general southern words that are so much a part of the Ocracoke dialect, as well as a sampling of the northern terms that help to give the largely southern-flavored Ocracoke vocabulary its distinctive island spice.

OCRACOKE VOCABULARY LIST

abreast (prep.): Across from. Although this word has a different meaning ('side by side') in many other dialects, the use of *abreast* to mean 'across from' comes from nautical usage and is found mostly in coastal areas ("The boats were abreast the lighthouse").

across the beach (prep. phr.): On the beach by the sea ("Did you see the shark that washed up across the beach?").

addled (adj.): Dazed or confused. A general southern term ("John was addled").

airish (adj.): Chilly and breezy ("After that squall came through, it was right airish out").

away (adv.): At a different location. Used with the verb *live* to refer to someone who has lived off the island for a period ("She lived away for a while after she first got married").

back of the island (n.): The part of the island located on the sound side, from the Coast Guard station toward Hammock Hill ("He fished on the back of the island").

Banker (n.): A person living on the Outer Banks islands off the coast of North Carolina. This term was used as early as the mid-1700s, primarily by mainland North Carolinians. It is rare on Ocracoke ("She talks like a Banker").

begombed (adj.): To be soiled, usually with a sticky or greasy residue ("Ellen's shirt was begombed with paint").

breakwater (v.): To set up a barrier to stop the forces of water, as before a harbor ("They breakwatered that area by Oyster Creek").

breeze up (v.): To get windy ("Shut the windows; it's breezing up outside").

buck (n.): A friend, usually a male friend ("He's a real buck").

bucky (n.): Same as *buck*, used primarily in direct address ("Hey bucky, what you doin'?").

call the mail over (v. phr.): Distribute the mail. Comes originally from the custom of calling aloud the names of those who received letters at the dock when the mail boat arrived. Now used for more general reference to the distribution of mail in the boxes at the post office ("Is the mail called over yet?").

carry (v.): To take, bring, escort, accompany. A general southern term that is now fairly common on Ocracoke ("Would you carry me to school?").

cat (n.): An island version of baseball in which fielders may put batters out by throwing the ball at them, as in dodge ball. Sticks and homemade versions of balls (for example, crumpled aluminum foil) were typically used in playing this game ("We played cat a lot when we were kids").

catawampus (adj.): In a diagonal position, crooked, not square. A fairly general colloquial term, used mainly in the South ("The boxes in the general store were piled up all catawampus"). Also *cattywampus*.

chuck (v.): Wedge, force apart ("Chuck the door open a little").

chunk (v.): To throw, particularly natural objects such as rocks or sticks. General southern term ("Chunk the rock in the water").

Co-cola (n.): A soft drink. Used for the trademark drink *Coca-Cola* or, by extension, for any carbonated drink. This general southern term is used as a single word and results from the loss of the unaccented syllable *-ca* in *Cóca-Cóla* ("Would you like a Co-cola?").

comforter (n.): Bedspread or quilt. This northern pronunciation contrasts with the mainland southern version, *comfort* ("Cathy got another comforter, because she was still cold").

counterpane (n.): Bedspread. Only used by elderly Ocracokers now ("My mother tucked the counterpane under the pillow").

creek (n.): A small inlet running from the sound through the island or into the island. The word *creek* often occurs in the proper names for these inlets, as in Oyster Creek. The term *the Creek* refers to the main harbor, Silver Lake ("What were all those dingbatters doing over to the Creek the other day?").

Creeker (n.): A person who lives or was raised in the area by Silver Lake, or the Creek, particularly as opposed to someone who lives by the Point. At one time, there may have been a social division between Creekers and Pointers ("I've been a Creeker all my life").

cut on/off (v.): Switch, turn off or on. General southern usage ("Please cut off the lights when you leave the room").

dingbatter (n.): A nonnative of Ocracoke or the Outer Banks. Sometimes used somewhat negatively to refer to someone who is ignorant of island life ("The dingbatter kept getting his fishing line tangled with mine").

ditch (n.): The mouth of a harbor. *The Ditch* refers to the mouth of Silver Lake Harbor ("Did you see that skiff by the Ditch?").

doast (n.): A cold, influenza ("I got a doast"). Also a large amount ("James Barrie caught a doast of crabs today").

doasted (adj.): Feeling sick, typically with influenza ("Don't get near me today; I'm doasted").

down below (adv.): The area north of Ocracoke Village, between the beginning of the National Park and Hatteras ("Rex is goin' down below to see the wild ponies").

down Creek/Base, etc. (adv.): The term *down* may be used with a variety of geographical terms to indicate specific locations on Ocracoke Island. For example, *down Creek* refers to the main part of the village by Silver Lake, *down Base* refers to the Coast Guard base, and so forth ("Charlene went down Creek for a Co-cola").

down Sound (adv.): Located to the south of Ocracoke, in the Core Sound area—for example, Cedar Island or Harkers Island ("Rex and Beach went down Sound for the day").

ebb tide (n.): Low tide. A general nautical term ("Ebb tide was at 6:30 this morning").

ever been (adv.): Ever existed, ever been witnessed ("That's the nicest flounder that's ever been").

face 'n' eyes (n.): Face, often used with derision ("Get out of my face! I don't want to see your face 'n' eyes until nine-thirty!").

family (n.): Relatives, including immediate and extended family members. This usage now alternates with the more general southern *kin(wfolk)* ("We got family in Salter Path").

fatback (n.): An Outer Banks term for menhaden, an oily fish used for fertilizer and cosmetics ("We sure got a big catch of fatback last month").

fetch up (v.): Appear, show up. From the more common term *fetch* meaning 'get' ("He finally fetched up after taking a cruise").

fixin' to (v.): About to do something or to plan or intend to do something. A widespread southern term ("They're fixin' to go down below").

fladget (n.): A piece of something. Used mostly in reference to food or wounds ("He cut a fladget of skin off his finger").

flood tide (n.): High tide. General nautical term ("I sure hope that hurricane doesn't arrive at flood tide").

for sure (adj.): Certain, definite. A common term in most dialects of American English, but unusual on Ocracoke for its placement within the sentence ("He's for sure about the meeting").

for to (prep.): In order to ("She came for to visit").

foreigner (n.): An off-islander. Generally only used by the oldest residents now, having been replaced by *dingbatter* ("He lives on the island, but he's a foreigner").

frigidaire (n.): Refrigerator. This broadening of the meaning of the word for a particular brand of refrigerator to include all refrigerators is a general southern usage ("The Co-cola's in the frigidaire").

goaty (adj.): Foul-smelling. From the bad smell of a goat ("Get away from me; you're smelling goaty").

going at (v.): Going to ("Are you going at the Pub tonight?").

goodsome (adj.): Very good. *Some* can be attached to a variety of different adjectives to intensify the quality of the adjective (*badsome, prettysome*). The adjective it attaches to, however, can be of one or two syllables only. For example, one cannot say "The cat is beautifulsome," but one can say "That meal was goodsome." The adjective that *some* attaches to typically occurs at the end of the phrase, so that one says "He was uglysome" but not "He was an uglysome man."

guano (n.): Fertilizer, often from fowl such as chickens or coastal birds. By extension, it can refer to any type of fertilizer, including commercial fertilizer. Comes from the Spanish term *guano* (from Peru), where it was used to refer to dung from coastal birds. Typically pronounced as *go-ANN-a* or *go-ANN-er* on Ocracoke ("Did Owen put enough goanna on his garden?").

gutful (n.): A full stomach, typically from eating ("Rex had a gutful of food last night").

haint (n.): A ghost ("Some people think they've seen haints on the island"). Also an older pronunciation of the negative verb *ain't* when used in an accented position in a sentence ("Háin't that nice that y'all have come back to visit us!").

hammock (n.): A grove of trees. On Ocracoke, this word is incorporated into the name of an island location, Hammock Hill. Older usage ("Let's go on down to Hammock Hill").

hard blow (n.): A strong wind ("We had a real hard blow last weekend").

Hatterasser (n.): A person from Hatteras ("I think she's a native Hatterasser").

hear tell (v.): Hear. General southern rural usage ("I hear tell that Blackbeard was killed on Ocracoke").

heist (v.): To lift, raise. An older pronunciation of *hoist* ("She heisted the window because it was too warm in here").

hill (n.): Dune; that is, a sand hill or sand ridge. May be used as part of place names on Ocracoke ("Let's ride up to Hammock Hill").

kin(folk) (n.): Relatives. General southern usage ("They're kin to me").

Kinnykeeter (n.): A person from an area near Avon, which used to be called Kinnakeet. Used somewhat negatively in the phrase "Kinnykeeter yaupon eater." See *yaupon*.

lay a cussin' on (v. phr.): To swear at someone ("She's gonna lay a cussin' on him").

liable to (adv.): Likely, apt to. A widespread colloquial term ("She's liable to run when she sees you").

lighter wood (n.): Kindling ("We got some lighter wood in the yard").

listen at (v.): Listen to ("She was listening at David last night").

louard (adv.): Going away from the wind. Derives from the nautical term *lee-ward* ("The boat was going louard during the storm").

mainland (n.): The non-island parts of the United States, particularly North Carolina, as opposed to the Outer and Core Banks ("That new family is from the mainland").

mash (v.): To press, smash. General southern usage ("Jane mashed the wrong button on her computer; Daddy mashed his toe in the door").

meddlin' (v.): Interfering. General southern usage ("They were meddlin' in my business").

meehonkey (n.): A game of hide-and-seek played by earlier generations of children on Ocracoke Island, or a call used while playing this game. What distinguishes the Ocracoke version of hide-and-seek from the usual variety is the huge area the game encompasses—not just one family's backyard but often a large area within the village. To make the game more fair to seekers, children would make noises while hiding; *meehonkey* was the usual call. This word probably comes in part from the imitation of a goose call ("We used to play meehonkey every evening in the summertime").

miserable'n the wind (adj. phr.): Agitated, feeling very uneasy or unsettled. Very bad. A shortened version of the phrase *miserabler than the wind* ("Rudy is miserable'n the wind when he's on his week off from the ferry; the day was miserable'n the wind").

mommuck (v.): To harass or bother. In Shakespeare's day, this term had a rather different meaning: to break, cut, or tear into fragments or shreds. The sentence "Young'uns, hain't I been mommucked this day!" is an island classic that includes several recognized traditional dialect traits, of which the use of *mommuck* is the most prominent. Also *mammock, mammick*.

mommuckin' (n.): Beating, harassment ("He got a mommuckin' from his brothers").

nor'easter (n.): A storm from the north and east, generally quite powerful. This is a general term along the Atlantic Coast ("The worst storms are the nor'easters"). Also *sou'easter*.

no tellin' (adv.): No way of knowing. This is a general southern usage ("There's no tellin' what he might do").

O'cocker (n.): A person born and raised on Ocracoke, a native as opposed to a nonnative resident. Pronounced as *OH-cock-er*, it is a shortened form of *Ocracoker*. The term is generally used only by native Ocracokers ("Kenny is an O'cocker").

Ocracoke (n.): The name of the island, probably derived originally from the Algonquian word *waxihikami*, meaning 'enclosed place or fort'. Through misspelling and English-like pronunciation, the word became *Wococon* and, eventually, *Ocracoke*. In one popular island legend, *Ocracoke* comes from the phrase, "Oh, crow cock," which was spoken by the infamous pirate Blackbeard as he waited to do battle at sunrise with the governor's forces who had come to capture him.

of a/the morning/evening, etc. (adv. phr.): In the morning, mornings. Times of the day or seasons of the year may be used with the preposition *of*, as in *of the fall* instead of *in the fall*. Now typically used only by the oldest residents ("We would go hunting of the morning").

off-island (adj.): Not from the island ("Walt is an off-island person who studies dialects"). Also a prepositional phrase meaning 'currently not at home on the island' ("Dave is off-island today").

offshore (adj.): Crazy, silly or outlandish. A metaphorical extension of the literal use of the term *offshore* ("Those dingbatters are offshore"). If someone is particularly outlandish, Ocracokers might say "He's offshore and can't get back in."

on account of (conj.): Because. Widespread term in a number of dialects ("He's off the island this winter on account of the cold").

on-island (adj.): Presently on the island ("I think she's on-island today").

over to the beach (prep. phr.): At the beach, by the ocean ("Ike is over to the beach").

penning (n.): Rounding up and corralling into a fenced area or pen ("We had a pony penning once a year").

pizer (n.): A porch on a house. From Italian *piazza*. Used only by older speakers now ("We sat on the pizer and watched the young'uns").

Pointer (n.): A person who lives at the southern tip of the residential area called the Point. At one time, the social division separating a Pointer from a Creeker may have been significant in terms of status.

poke sack (n.): A sack or bag. General southern use ("Did you put the duck in the poke sack?").

puck (n.): A sweetheart. Generally used by middle-aged and younger people. Also generally used by women or to refer to women ("Melinda is his puck").

quamished (adj.): Sick to the stomach. This term comes from *qualmish*, which means prone to qualms or spells of sickness, and is found in Shakespeare and even earlier writings ("I felt quamished on the ferry").

reckon (v.): To guess or suppose. A general southern usage ("I reckon it'll be cold by then").

right (adv.): Very, really. Intensifies the quality of an adjective or adverb. A general southern usage ("She's a right nice person").

right many (adj.): A lot. General southern expression ("She took right many pictures of her").

Russian rat (n.): A large rodent found on Ocracoke, technically known as a *nutria* ("We have lots of Russian rats and mink on the island").

sack (n.): Paper bag. General southern usage. Usually replaced by *bag* on Ocracoke, but still used to a limited extent by older speakers. This term is often used as part of the expression *tab the sack*, which refers to a practice at the general store in which an account to be paid at a later time is recorded on a paper *bag/sack* ("Do you want me to tab the sack?").

say a word (v.): To talk a lot ("Those men to the store sure can say a word").

scud (n.): A ride, usually in a car. Can also be used on occasion for a ride in a boat ("Candy took a scud around the island").

scuttle (n.): A hole in a wall or roof covered by a door. Also used for the hatch on the deck or sides of a boat ("We used to hide in that scuttle when we were little").

skeeter (n.): Mosquito. This specialized pronunciation has become a word in its own right, both on Ocracoke and throughout the South in general ("Ocracoke has some large skeeters").

skeeter hawk (n.): Dragonfly. Also, a large mosquito-like insect that eats mosquitoes, alternately known as the crane fly ("Jen opened the window to let a skeeter hawk outside").

skiff (n.): A small, light boat that can be sailed or rowed by one person. A widespread nautical term ("He doesn't fish in the skiff").

slick cam (n.): A very calm water, typically used with reference to the sound ("It was a slick cam out there today"). *Cam* is pronounced so that it rhymes with *ram*. Also *slick calm*.

smidget (n.): A small piece, sliver, usually referring to food ("Candy took a smidget of cake"). Compare the term *smidgen* in other dialects.

stay the night/day, etc. (v. phr.): Stay for the night. A widespread expression in a number of dialects ("Marge stayed the night on the island").

'tall (adv.): At all. A specialized, older pronunciation that has become a word in its own right ("They don't like her 'tall").

tell a yarn (v. phr.): Exaggerate a story, make up a story ("That man can sure tell a yarn").

this day (adv.): Today. Typically refers to something that will take place before the day is completed ("You'll be punished this day").

to (prep.): Located in a particular place; generally used where *at* is used in other dialects ("Rena Dell is over to the restaurant").

token (n.): A sign or presage of something to come; an omen or portent, often referring to death. This use of *token* dates back to Old English ("The haint was a token of death").

tote (v.): Carry. A general southern usage ("Did she tote the stuff over here?").

tote sack (n.): A bag for carrying items ("Jen brought it in a tote sack").

turn out (v.): Dismiss, let out ("The principal turned out school because of the flooding").

upside (prep.): On the side of, alongside. This is a general southern term ("She hit him upside the head").

up the beach (adv.): North of Ocracoke—for example, Hatteras, Nags Head, or Norfolk ("Dave is going up the beach this weekend").

wampus cat (n.): A fictitious cat invoked to scare and tease children. Used on Ocracoke to refer to someone who is abnormal in some respect, possibly to someone especially silly or especially heavy. It may be derived from a creative inversion of *catawampus* ("Walt's a classic example of an off-island wampus cat").

water fire (n./v.): Light that appears on the surface of a body of swampy water at night, caused by gases released by decaying plant matter. In Ocracoke, the appearance of water fire traditionally is associated with poor fishing on the following day ("Last night the water fire; no fish today").

whipstitch (n.): Every now and then, sporadically. From the term *whipstitch* used in sewing for a stitch that threads over and again in a spiral formation. Used now mostly by older speakers ("Those linguists come around here every whipstitch").

whit (n.): A considerable period of time, a bit of time. The meaning of this word has been extended to refer to bits of time from its older English usage to refer to small bits of things ("He's been gone a whit now").

whoop and holler (n.): A game of hide-and-seek played by earlier generations of children on Ocracoke Island. See *meehonkey*, which was the more common term among older residents ("Back in those days we used to play whoop and holler of the evenin'").

winard (adv.): Windward, into the wind ("We have a better catch going winard").

y'all (pron.): Plural of *you*. This is a general southern term used widely on Ocracoke ("Y'all have a nice day").

yaupon, yapan (n.): A small evergreen shrub related to the holly that grows in sandy soil. It can be used in making a medicinal herb tea often employed to induce vomiting ("Did you have some yaupon tea?").

yet (adv.): Still. Used with this meaning only by older people now. A similar use is found in Irish English and a few small dialect areas in England ("Blanche eats a lot of fish yet").

yonder (adv.): More distant, further. A general southern usage ("The boat is over yonder").

young'uns (n.): Young children. A general southern expression, particularly in rural dialect areas where older pronunciations are retained ("The young'uns don't like the same games we played in our day").

Sounding Like a "Hoi Toider"

3

On our first visit to Ocracoke a few years ago, Walt Wolfram was introduced to a group of men in the midst of a typical island party—in this instance, the celebration of an islander's retirement from the Coast Guard. As an outsider, Walt felt awkward, but he was honored to be included in this locals-only event on just our second day on the island. He only knew one islander at the party, Dave Esham, who introduced Walt as the leader of a research team who had come to study Ocracoke speech—an obvious outsider. Walt's discomfort as an intrusive dingbatter had nearly peaked when a friendly, curly-haired man by the name of Rex O'Neal stepped forward and said in a good-natured tone: "So you're here studyin' speech. Well, it's hoi toide on the saind soide. Last night the water far, tonight the moon shine. No feesh."

Everyone present laughed at the performance, which highlighted the importance of distinctive pronunciations in the Ocracoke brogue. Since that time, we

Walt Wolfram laughs
heartily at an islander's
joke. (Photograph by
Herman Lankford)

have heard this "performance phrase" and have encountered the distinctive pronunciation traits associated with the dialect on a regular basis, but this initial
utterance provided an inspirational moment. It was the phrase that first focused
our attention on the characteristic pronunciations that are an integral part of
Ocracoke English.

In this chapter, we describe some of the major pronunciation features of the
traditional brogue, as well as the ways in which these features are changing.
First, though, we should say something about the overall impression that the

Rex O'Neal shares some island phrases with Walt Wolfram and
Natalie Schilling-Estes. (Photograph by Herman Lankford)

sounds of the brogue convey to outsiders and to islanders. As it turns out, the
impressions of outsiders are partly responsible for the way islanders have come
to view their own speech. Islanders realize that their speech is often a topic of
conversation among tourists, and just about all native Ocracokers can relate
stories about visitors who identified themselves as tourists by calling attention
to Ocracoke speech. The worst dingbatters will directly solicit speech from the
local residents, perhaps by saying something like, "Talk for us so we can hear
how you speak." Others will more subtly, but quite noticeably, engage islanders
in empty chatter just to hear the sound of their voices.

Ocracokers also get reactions to their speech from outsiders when they travel off the island, whether their destinations are relatively nearby mainland areas
such as Greenville, North Carolina, or Norfolk, Virginia, or overseas locations

in Europe, particularly England. The brogue elicits a wide range of comments from people trying to guess where it comes from, but most first-time listeners think it is decidedly non-American, probably an unspecified dialect from the British Isles or Australia. As Candy Gaskill, as well-known islander, put it, "I work in the store [Albert Styron's General Store] and they [visitors] say, 'Well, are you from Australia?' or 'Are you from England?'" Chester Lynn, an Ocracoker who works in the island's Variety Store, reported that he fooled fellow travelers (mostly Americans) in England for half a day by declaring that his distinct speech was a southern British dialect: "I went on a trip to Europe one time, and we met in London. And some people in London, when they met some other people from the United States that had been in London, they thought that I was from London. And so for a joke we went and told them I was from outside of London, and they believed it for half the trip."

According to islanders, visitors from England and Australia have also said that the Ocracoke brogue sounds more like British or Australian English than do mainland American dialects, thus encouraging the belief that Ocracokers speak some sort of British-sounding dialect. When we first heard about tourists who thought that Ocracoke speech sounded British, we were a little skeptical, but, as it turns out, these tourists might have been right. On one of our visits to Ocracoke, we brought along a famous British dialectologist, Peter Trudgill. He was amazed at how much the dialect sounded like some of the British dialects he had studied in the course of his lengthy career. Intrigued by the similarities, he took several Ocracoke speech samples back to England with him. A couple of months later, he sent us the results of an experiment he had conducted with a group of British listeners in Essex:

A group of 15 native speakers of British English were played a tape consisting of five different speakers from five different parts of the English-speaking world, and asked to identify the origins of the speakers. Although very successful in most cases, they were unanimous in allocating an origin in England to the Ocracoke speaker, with most people opting for an origin in "the West Country"—that is, southwestern England—although two suggested East Anglia, and one Derbyshire.

Candy Gaskill and Chester Lynn chat outside Albert Styron's General Store. (Photograph by Ann Sebrell Ehringhaus)

To a large extent, the association of the Ocracoke brogue with British English comes from the classic pronunciation of the *i* vowel as something like *oy* in words like *hoi toide* for 'high tide'. Some British dialects have a similar-sounding *i* vowel. These include Cockney, a London dialect, and the dialect spoken in Devon in southwestern England. Other British vowels also remind us of the Ocracoke *i* sound. For example, in some parts of Britain, words with *ay* vowels, such as *say* and *raid*, may be pronounced almost like the Ocracoke words *sigh* and *ride*.

Other Ocracoke pronunciations, too, may strike the listener as British. For example, Ocracokers pronounce the name *Hatteras* with a British-like *t* sound in the middle, so that it comes out something like *Hat-tris*, whereas most mainland Americans would say *Hadderis*. Similarly, the Ocracoke *aw* sound, as in *call*, may strike a listener as very similar to pronunciations found in parts of England where words like *ball* and *fall* sound almost like *bull* and *full*.

Some of the same qualities of Ocracoke English that lead listeners to think it sounds British may also persuade them that it sounds Australian. In Australian speech, the *i* in *time* and *tide* sounds something like the Ocracoke vowel of *hoi toide*, as does the *ay* in *mate* or *say*, unless we exaggerate this pronunciation (as most people do who try to imitate stereotypical Australian English) so that *mate* sounds like *might* and *say* like *sigh*.

Although the claim that Ocracoke English is equivalent to British or Australian English may be exaggerated, it has served a useful social role in elevating the status of the brogue. The characteristic pronunciations of the Ocracoke brogue are now viewed positively by many islanders, who are regularly told that their accent sounds like a quaint variety of British or Australian English, both of which are highly valued in contrast to most American English dialects. In previous generations, the Outer Banks brogue was typically denounced as substandard English, but at present its stature is growing.

Today, there is even a hint of pride discernible as islanders discuss gatherings where the brogue becomes so thick that others cannot follow it. For example, James Barrie Gaskill, an O'cocker who owns Albert Styron's General Store, proudly told us that it took his mainland father-in-law ten years to be able to understand his new son-in-law's accent. And island men who regularly play poker together report that even their wives have trouble understanding what they are saying during the heat of these games. Although these claims might seem slightly exaggerated, they are not put forward apologetically. Instead, islanders note with pride—and perhaps a touch of scorn for uncomprehending outsiders—that they are the only ones who can really speak and understand the Ocracoke brogue at its thickest.

SOUNDING LIKE AN O'COCKER

Before we begin this section on some details related to the pronunciations of the Ocracoke brogue, a word of caution is in order. We have tried to present these pronunciations without becoming overly technical and without resorting to the use of the International Phonetic Alphabet, a special universal alphabet designed to capture precisely any human speech sound regardless of the language or dialect. For example, if we were to write out a word like *tide* as it is pronounced on Ocracoke, using this phonetic alphabet and all its nuances, it would look something like [tʰʌⱨːⁱd] rather than *toide*, as we represent it here. Such phonetic precision makes perfect sense to a handful of linguists scattered across the globe, but it is totally incomprehensible to most people who just want to know something about the pronunciation of the brogue. So we have used slightly modified English spellings to convey the approximate pronunciations. Interested readers can get a better feel for the actual pronunciations that characterize the Ocracoke brogue by listening to some of the speakers on the archival tapes available through the North Carolina Language and Life Project at North Carolina State University.

The *I* Vowel: "It's Hoi Toide on the Sound Soide"

When outsiders—and islanders—refer to Ocracokers as "hoi toiders," they are seizing upon the most noticeable feature of the Outer Banks brogue: the unique pronunciation of the *i* vowel. People often think this vowel is pronounced just like the *oy* in *boy* or *toy*, but that is a slight exaggeration. In reality, the typical Ocracoke *i* has its roots in the *i* sound that was common in the Early Modern English period, when the first settlers arrived on Ocracoke. Back in the early 1700s, the *i* in words like *tide* was rendered like the *uh* in *but* followed very quickly by *ee* as in *beat*, giving us *h-uh-ee* for *high* and *t-uh-ee-d* for *tide*. Over time, the *i* vowel changed drastically in most varieties of American English, becoming *ah* plus *ee* in nonsouthern varieties and just plain *ah* in the South (as in *tahm* for *time*). On Ocracoke, the Early Modern English *uh-ee* didn't change quite as drastically, because the island was so isolated from the mainland. Today, Ocracokers still pronounce *i* almost like *uh-ee*, although with a bit more of an *oy* sound than in Early Modern English times. But the Ocracoke *i* isn't exactly an *oy*. In fact, Ocracokers point out that they only pronounce their *i*'s as *oy*'s when they're exaggerating to make the tourists happy.

As we shall see, the *i* vowel is by no means the only pronunciation feature that sets Ocracokers apart from mainlanders. So why is it that this one feature always captures the spotlight when people comment on the Outer Banks brogue? One important reason is that Ocracoke *oy* serves as an excellent marker of islander identity because it contrasts so sharply with the sound of standard English *i*, and even more sharply with mainland southern *ah*. When we hear someone say "What t*ah*m is it?" for "What t*i*me is it?" or "The t*ah*d is h*ah*" for "The t*i*de is h*i*gh," we automatically identify that person as having southern roots. Similarly, when we hear "The *toide* is *hoi*," we associate the speaker with such coastal regions as the Outer Banks or Smith and Tangier Islands in the Chesapeake Bay.

Ocracokers capitalize on the distinctiveness of their *i* vowel when they wish to assert their identity as islanders. Sometimes they consciously add more *oy*'s into their speech, as Rex O'Neal does when he utters his "performance phrase" for curious tourists and language scholars. Often, though, islanders use the *oy* unconsciously as a way of setting themselves apart from mainlanders. For example, in an interview with one of our fieldworkers, Rex hardly used any *oy*'s at all. Instead, he tended to pronounce his *i*'s simply as *i*; probably he subconsciously wanted to speak as close to standard English as possible because he was being interviewed by a language expert. At one point during this interview, however, several of Rex's brothers drove up, and the men conducted a short conversation that did not include the fieldworker. Suddenly, Rex began using a lot more *oy*'s in his speech. It is very unlikely that this switch to the traditional Ocracoke pronunciation was the result of a conscious effort on Rex's part, as it would be very difficult indeed to concentrate on what you were saying if you constantly worried about how you were pronouncing each and every vowel. Rather, Rex quite unconsciously began using more *oy*'s than *i*'s because he identifies so strongly with his brothers as fellow family members—and fellow O'-cockers.

It may seem far-fetched to think that such subtle differences in pronunciation can be used to convey important social meanings. But this link between language and society is by no means confined to the brogue. All of us have been in situations where we suddenly find ourselves pronouncing words more carefully than we usually do on a day-to-day basis—perhaps during a job interview or in a meeting with a government official or teacher. Conversely, we may pro-nounce words far more casually at home than we do while we're at work or school. We may also notice that our pronunciations become more strongly accented when we're talking to people with whom we closely identify or with whom we want to fit in. Rarely do we make a conscious decision to change the way we speak—it just happens when we switch social settings. Such unconscious shifts are exactly what we find in Ocracoke English. Traditional pronunciations are used more often when O'cockers want to sound like O'cockers, whereas less "broguelike" sounds creep in when it's not as important to sound like an islander.

We have also noticed that the way Ocracokers pronounce their *i*'s depends not only on the particular social setting but even on which words they're using. In certain words that have strong associations with island life, such as *high* and *tide*, one rarely ever hears a non-*oy* vowel like the southern *ah*, while words that don't mean as much to Ocracokers may be pronounced in a more southern mainland manner. For example, some Ocracokers who otherwise use lots of *oy* vowels tend to say *ah* when they're talking about Carol*ah*na, the mainland portion of the state where people pronounce their *i*'s that way.

How islanders pronounce their *i*'s is also closely related to their ages. Young Ocracokers use the *oy* pronunciation far less than older islanders. However, as we already noted in Chapter 1, young Ocracokers don't use the southern *ah* nearly as much as we might think they would, given that they come into contact with mainland southerners on a daily basis. Instead, they tend to replace their *oy*'s with northern-sounding *ay*'s, partly because there are a number of northerners living on Ocracoke today, but also—and largely—because young Ocracokers are just as proud of their island identity as are their older relatives. Even though the traditional brogue is not an innate part of their speech, young islanders still seek, consciously or unconsciously, to keep themselves distinct from mainland southerners. Thus they avoid the southern *ah*, as well as other mainland southern dialect features, despite the fact that they're often surrounded by southern-sounding speech.

The Pronunciation of *Ar* for *Ire*

There is one group of words in which Ocracokers use much more of the southern-sounding *ah* for *i* than usual: words in which the *i* vowel is followed by an *r*, as in *far* for *fire* or *tar* for *tire*. This pronunciation is also found in dialect areas little influenced by southern *ah*, and even speakers who routinely say *oy* for *i* tend to change *oy* to *ah* before *r* sounds. Perhaps this dialect feature has resulted not so much from contact with southern speakers, but from considerations of ease or naturalness in pronunciation. Many speakers think of words like *tire* and *fire* as being one syllable long. Using the standard long-*i* vowel, however, it is practically impossible to pronounce these words without breaking them into two syllables sounding something like *tye-er* and *fye-er*. That is probably why speakers in several dialect regions, whether or not they are familiar with the southern *ah*, have independently ended up using *ah* before *r* as a way to preserve the single-syllable pronunciations of such words.

As further proof that the *ah* before *r* sound owes little to southern influence on Ocracoke, we can look at what islanders say to let people know that they're islanders rather than mainland southerners. For example, the second sentence in the "performance phrase" quoted earlier includes the pronunciation of *far* for *fire*: "Last night the water *far*." Similarly, when a young member of a long-established island family, Cathy Scarborough, was telling us about the experiences she and her friend, Melinda Jackson, had at college on the North Carolina mainland, she related a story in which the Outer Banks pronunciation of the word *fire* played a major part:

> They elected us to be the fire marshals for that floor. And what we were supposed to do if there was a fire in the dorm, if the fire alarm went off, was run around, knock on all the doors and say, "Fire, fire!" And make sure everybody could get out. Well, we got laughing, because have you ever heard Melinda say *fire*? "Far, far, far!" And Daddy and everybody told her if she runs around hollering that, won't nobody know what in the world she's talking about anyway.

So, in our discussion of the pronunciation characteristics of the Ocracoke dialect, it seems that we must divide the *i* sound into two groups: the *ah* we hear in words ending in *ire* and the *oy* we hear in other words. Most of the time, *oy* is considered the pronunciation by which people are identified as islanders; in *ire-* words, however, *ah* is good Outer Banks English.

The Sound of Ocracoke "Sound"

Despite the fact that the *hoi toide* sound seems to capture everyone's attention when they talk about the brogue, there are a number of other distinctive vowel sounds that more subtly act to set the brogue apart from other dialects of American English. One of these is the Ocracoke pronunciation of *ow*, as in *town* or *sound*, as more of an *ay* as in *say*, so that *town* sounds like *tain* and *sound* like *saind*. What we hear in these words isn't exactly an *ay*, just as what we hear in *i-* words isn't really *oy*. Rather, the Ocracoke *ow* is actually two sounds spoken quickly together, just like the *i* sound. To pronounce the *ow* like an islander, you need to say *eh* as in *bet*, followed by *ee* as in *beet*. Thus *sound* comes out sounding like *s-eh-ee-nd*, while *town* sounds like *t-eh-ee-n*—almost like *saind* and *tain*, but not quite.

Ocracoke *ow* is so difficult to capture with familiar spellings for the same reason that *i* also eludes written description. Both sounds evolved from older English sounds that we don't use—or write down—anymore. In most of today's English dialects, *ow* is made up of two sounds: *ah* as in *father*, plus *oo* as in *boot*. In the Early Modern English Period, when Ocracoke was settled, *ow* sounded like *uh* plus *oo*, so that *town* was pronounced *t-uh-oo-n*—sort of a cross between *tone* and *tune*. This old-fashioned pronunciation can still be heard in the Virginia Tidewater area, from which many of Ocracoke's first families came. The sound has changed on Ocracoke, but in a different way than it has in the rest of the country. The Ocracoke *ow* is living proof that even the most isolated dialects change over time, even if the changes they undergo are very different from those that take place in other areas. The *ow* sound provides us with direct evidence that Ocracoke English is not the language of Shakespeare—but it's certainly not the language of mainland America, either.

Fraysh Feesh and Other *Ih* and *Eh* Sound Patterns

One of the characteristic traits of the Ocracoke brogue is the pronunciation of the vowel in words like *fish* and *dish* as *ee*, so that *fish* sounds like *feesh* and *dish* like *deesh*. Most islanders think of this pronunciation as a classic feature of the traditional brogue, although in reality it is a trait shared by many southern mainland dialects as well. In fact, it is possible to hear this pronunciation more in some mainland areas than on the island.

It is hard to tell exactly why this general southern dialect feature has become identified with the stereotypical brogue; perhaps it is because the word *feesh* is used so frequently in Ocracoke, giving people plenty of opportunity to notice its pronunciation. Or perhaps the feature is so noticeable because, as even the oldest Ocracokers can attest, for years teachers have been correcting students who say *feesh*, insisting that they use the more standard *fish*. Because of the (largely negative) attention the word has received over the years, some islanders have become quite adept at shifting between *feesh* and *fish*, depending on who they are talking to or the effect they are trying to create. In guarded conversation with outsiders, islanders may say *fish*, but in casual conversation with friends they will more likely say *feesh*. And islanders putting on a performance for dingbatters who insist on hearing their speech may use the *ee* sound in words like *fish* and *dish* more than they normally would. So even though Ocracokers have yet to be referred to as *feeshermen* rather than *hoi toiders*, the use of *feesh* for *fish* does play a symbolic role similar to the use of *oy* for *i* in the projection of islander identity.

This same *ee* sound appears not just before the *sh*, but also before the *tch* sound as well, as in *deetch* for *ditch* and *keetchen* for *kitchen*. In many parts of the mainland South, *ee* for *ih* is much more widespread, resulting in *deeg* for *dig* and *beed* for *bid*. The pronunciation is also found before *l*, so that *pill* sounds almost like *peel* and *fill* like *feel*. A following *l* also affects words with *u* sounds, with *pull* and *pool* being pronounced almost identically. However, these differences in vowel pronunciations before *l* are not nearly as common in Ocracoke speech as they are on the mainland.

The *ih* sound is not the only one to be affected by a following *sh* in both

Ocracoke and mainland southern speech. The *eh* vowel (as in *fresh* and *mesh*) can come out like more of an *ay* (as in *say* or *day*) or even *i* (as in *fry* or *my*) when it occurs before *sh*. Thus *fresh* ends up sounding like *fraysh*, while *mesh* sounds like *maysh*. Similarly, when the vowel we hear in words like *put* and *foot* occurs before the *sh*, it sounds more like *oo*, as in *poosh* for *push* or *cooshion* for *cushion*.

Some linguists claim that the *feesh/fish* transition is a relatively new development in the English language, one that is under way in the American South but hasn't yet reached the North (if, in fact, it will ever get there). But there is evidence that the *feesh* pronunciation has actually been present in the language for quite some time, and it may even be traceable to the British English that settlers brought with them to the American South. Today, we can hear *feesh* for *fish* in some of England's southern counties, such as Devon, Somerset, and Wiltshire, as well as in more northern areas of England such as Lancashire. The fact that we hear this sound, as well as other pronunciations like the *hoi toide* vowel, on both sides of the Atlantic suggests that Ocracoke vowels have more to do with the historical connections between the Outer Banks and the British Isles than with new developments. Further, the fact that even the oldest Ocracokers say *feesh* for *fish* suggests that this pronunciation on Ocracoke doesn't have much to do with recent linguistic changes on the American mainland. It is also probably not mere coincidence that we can hear *feesh* in other historically isolated areas in the southern U.S., including Appalachia and the Ozarks.

Another pronunciation pattern that Ocracoke has in common with the mainland South is the occasional conflation of *ih* and *eh*, so that words like *pin* and *pen* sometimes come out sounding the same. In one of our first interviews, we were told about a traditional island custom known as a "cattle penning." We were not sure whether the speaker meant that the cows were *pinned* or "branded" in some way to identify them, or enclosed in a pen—that is, *penned*. The identical or near-identical pronunciation of the *ih* and *eh* sounds has been a familiar characteristic of southern speech for decades. The pattern may date back even further on the Outer Banks, although it hasn't received as much attention there as in mainland southern dialects.

For those who have grown up distinguishing *pen* and *pin* by referring to them as *ink pen* and *stick pin*, while pronouncing them both as *pin*, little is lost in the identical pronunciations, because the context generally tells listeners which word is meant. In fact, pronouncing two or more different words in exactly the same way, as with *two*, *to*, and *too* or *their*, *there*, and *they're*, is a natural and relatively common phenomenon called *homophony*. No one seems to worry about the fact that *two* and *to* and *their* and *there* were once pronounced differently in English but are now pronounced the same, and we rarely, if ever, get these homophones (or homonyms) mixed up, except when we try to spell them. Similarly, most people who pronounce *pin* and *pen* the same way don't get the two words confused.

Unfortunately, several generations of southerners, including those on the Outer Banks and in Appalachia, have been taught that if they don't learn to pronounce words like *pin* and *pen* differently, no one will understand what they're talking about. Perhaps the worst part of the obsession with "correctly" pronouncing *pin* and *pen* is that differentiating the pronunciation of these two words is extremely difficult for anyone who grew up pronouncing them the same. In many instances, it is even difficult for teachers who have been told to "correct" their students.

Another special *eh* sound we hear on Ocracoke occurs before *r*, as in words like *there*, *where*, and *bear*, which come out sounding something like *thar*, *whar*, and *bar* in island speech. This pronunciation is not common in most southern mainland dialects, but we do hear it in some historically isolated dialect areas in the mountains. The reason for this particular pronunciation pattern is that when an *r* follows a vowel it can drastically alter the sound of the vowel. We have already seen how *r* turns the *i* vowel into *ah*, as in *far* for *fire*. It is not surprising that *r* has the same effect on *eh*, turning words like *bear* and *fair* into *bar* and *far*. So how can we tell what Ocracokers mean when they say *far*—are they saying *fire*, *fair*, or just plain *far*? Although there are subtle differences in the pronunciations of these three words, we usually have to depend on context to figure out which word is which. Luckily, few islanders go around saying things like "Is the fair fire far?" to see if outsiders can detect the small differences in the vowel sounds of these three words!

Ocracoke *R*

One of the classic features of traditional lowland southern dialects is the dropping of *r* after a vowel, either at the end of a word, as in *far* and *fear*, or before a consonant, as in *cart* or *fierce*. Thus, we expect to hear *fah* for *far* and *caht* for *cart* in the Piedmont and Coastal Plain regions of mainland North Carolina, and that is what we typically do encounter, at least in the speech of older mainlanders. But on Ocracoke, as in other Outer Banks communities, speakers traditionally have pronounced their *r*'s. That is, the typical islander of any age will say *far* and *fear* rather than *fah* and *feah*. In this respect, Ocracoke speech resembles most northern dialects, as well as highland southern dialects like Appalachian and Ozark English. The pronunciation of *r* on the Outer Banks once contrasted sharply with pronunciations on the neighboring mainland, and we can still hear a striking difference between the speech of older lifetime residents of Ocracoke and that of older people from a mainland area like Greenville or Raleigh, North Carolina. If we compare a younger Ocracoker with a young mainlander, though, we will not hear as much difference in the *r*'s. This is because younger mainland southerners are more likely to pronounce their *r*'s than their older relatives — particularly if they're Americans of European descent and are living in one of the more metropolitan areas of North Carolina, such as Raleigh, Wilmington, or Fayetteville.

Although Ocracoke is primarily an *r*-pronouncing dialect, certain words may trigger the dropping of the *r* sound. For example, in words like *yesterday* and *aggravate*, the *r* may be dropped because it occurs in an unaccented syllable, which is pronounced less forcefully than the syllables around it. Words like *yeste'day* and *agg'avate* have become classic markers of the Ocracoke brogue, and they often appear in the small dictionaries of Outer Banks words for sale in island gift shops. In truth, though, they are not unique to the island but are simply *r*-less pronunciations of common words that stand out because there is little "*r*-lessness" elsewhere in Ocracoke speech.

The *r* sound may also be dropped in unaccented syllables that fall at the ends of words, as in *brothuh* for *brother* and *Octobuh* for *October*. However, this final-*r* absence may not be very noticeable to outsiders who come from the mainland

South to listen to the brogue, because this type of *r*-lessness is nothing new to them. In fact, it's much more widespread in the mainland South than on Ocracoke or the rest of the Outer Banks.

Finally, on Ocracoke the *r* sometimes may be dropped after a consonant rather than a vowel. For example, the word *throw* may be pronounced as *th'o* and *threw* as *th'ew*. This type of *r*-dropping occurs only after the *th* and before *oh* and *oo* sounds and is widespread in the mainland South. The only other time an *r* is dropped after a consonant is in unstressed syllables (*p'ofessor* for *professor* or *p'oliferate* for *proliferate*), as mentioned above in the discussion of *agg'avate* and *yeste'day*.

Despite the presence of some limited *r*-dropping patterns in Ocracoke English, the brogue remains an unquestionably *r*-pronouncing dialect. In this regard, it is more similar to most northern speech than to traditional lowland southern dialects. The *r* sound also sets the brogue apart from the *r*-less dialects in New England and New York City, which have given rise to such stereotyped expressions as "Pahk the cah in Hahvahd Yahd" for "Park the car in Harvard Yard." Finally, the *r* serves to differentiate Ocracoke English from standard British English, or "received pronunciation," a dialect noteworthy for its *r*-lessness.

How can such a major difference between British English and Ocracoke English exist, given all the other similarities between these two dialects today, as well as the historical connection between them? To answer this question, we must clear up some common misconceptions about *r*-lessness in British English. First, not all dialects of British English are *r*-less. Some of the rural dialects in the southwest of England are *r*-pronouncing, as are some scattered dialects in the midland area. Irish English also pronounces the *r* in words like *farm*, *car*, and *fort*. Perhaps more important, and quite contrary to popular understanding, *r*-lessness has not always been the predominant and prestigious speech pattern in England.

Around 1700, when Ocracoke was first being settled, the limited *r*-lessness that existed in varieties of British English was associated with uneducated, rustic dialects rather than "the King's English." It was not until the end of the eighteenth century that the *r* began to drop out of elite speech. This was, of course, long after the departure of the people who would become the first European settlers on the Outer Banks. So the *r*-pronouncing dialect that characterizes the Outer Banks today, if it is indeed a reflection of the English and Irish-English roots of those original settlers, is an outgrowth of the "proper English" of the early 1700s — not of today's British received pronunciation.

One important lesson that we can learn from the history of *r* in American and British English is how fickle people can be in terms of the status they assign to particular pronunciations. Over the course of several centuries, a single trait can rise and fall in social standing time and time again, showing that there is nothing intrinsically "better" about certain pronunciations than others. Rather, a pronunciation acquires prestige when upper-class or educated speakers begin to favor it, and it can just as quickly lose its positive value when the social and cultural elites toss it aside.

British English speakers transformed the absence of *r* after a vowel from a token of uncultivated speech into a symbol of urbane sophistication about two hundred years ago. In America, we are now seeing an opposing movement in the status of *r*-lessness. In the American South before World War II, *r* dropping was associated with southern aristocracy. Nowadays, though, it is connected with rural, less educated southern speech. Similarly, in the New York City of a half-century ago, *r* dropping used to be prestigious. Today, though, it is so low on the social ladder that we consider it a stereotypical sign of working-class speech. In fact, pronunciations like *yohk* for *York*, *boid* for *bird*, and *fou'* for *four* may now be used for comical effect. The shifting status of *r* over the years shows us that it is not really how you pronounce something that counts, but who you are when you pronounce it. If you wait long enough, the "right people" can bestow status on just about any pronunciation. By the same token, the use of a language trait by the "wrong people" can stigmatize it regardless of previous associations.

Extry Skeeters on Ocracoke

Anyone who has ever visited Ocracoke during the hot, muggy part of the summer can certainly understand why *skeeters*, the local pronunciation for *mosquitoes*, is heard so often on the island. This form of the word even appears in print on souvenir T-shirts that depict an oversized skeeter proclaiming, "Send more tourists. The last batch was delicious!" This caption as a whole reflects the feelings of Ocracokers toward outsiders, who bring in money but also threaten the traditional way of life. In the same way, a single word or variant pronunciation, such as *skeeters*, can be used symbolically to project certain feelings about island cultural traditions. *Skeeters* is the product of two pronunciation patterns that were historically widespread in many dialects of English. Although these pronunciations are fading from use, particularly among younger Ocracokers, islanders still continue to use them in certain words, especially those that play a symbolic role in setting them apart from outsiders. In such cases, the older pronunciations often become so much a part of the words in which they still occur that they shape new words, complete with their own spellings.

One of the pronunciation patterns that gave rise to *skeeters* is the dropping of the first syllable of a word when that syllable is unaccented. We have already seen that the *r* sound in unstressed syllables may be lost, as in *brothuh* for *brother* and *agg'avate* for *aggravate*. Sometimes this process is extended, and entire unaccented syllables fall away. The disappearance of the *mo-* in *mosquito* may seem peculiar to nonsoutherners, but all English speakers occasionally drop unaccented syllables, whether in the middle of words (*sep'rate rooms* for *separate rooms*) or at the beginning (*'cause* for *because* or *How 'bout it* for *How about it*). In some dialects this very natural, widespread process extends to more words than usual. For example, in Ocracoke English, Appalachian English, and other rural southern dialects, unaccented syllable loss occurs in a wide range of words, so that we may hear *'taters* and *'maters* for *potatoes* and *tomatoes*, *'posed-ta* for *supposed to*, *'lectricity* for *electricity*, *'member* for *remember*, and, of course, *skeeters* for *mosquitoes*.

The second part of the *skeeter* pronunciation is due to a different dialect trait. When the last syllable of a word is an unaccented *-oh* or *-ow* sound, like the last syllable of *mosquito*, it may be pronounced as *-er*. This rule accounts for pronunciations such as *yeller*, *'tater*, *feller*, *winder* (for *window*), and so forth. This is a common rural pronunciation that has been popularized in books like *Old Yeller* and in expressions like *'maters and 'taters*.

Final *-oh* and *-ow* are not the only unaccented syllables that have special pronunciations in Ocracoke English. The final unaccented -*uh* in words like *extra*, *soda*, *Santa*, and *Virginia* may be pronounced as -*ee*, so that we hear *extry*, *sody*, *Santy*, and *Virginny*. This pattern is hardly unique to Ocracoke. Popular references to *Santy Claus* and songs like "Carry Me Back to Ole Virginny" show how widespread this pronunciation historically has been in the rural South.

Hain't That a *T* in "Doast"?

Islanders are typically very generous people who share easily. It was therefore not surprising when Elizabeth Howard, a knowledgeable and highly respected older O'cocker who could trace her island heritage to the original settlement of Ocracoke, told us she had a couple of gifts for us at the conclusion of our interview with her. Along with the gift of a jar of fig preserves from her well-stocked cupboards, she handed us a souvenir T-shirt that read "Young'uns, hain't I been mommucked this day!!!" Once again, an islander had beaten us to the punch by pointing out to us a peculiarity of Ocracoke pronunciation, as well as the Outer Banks word *mommuck*. One of the most noticeable island pronunciation features is the use of *hain't* for *ain't*.

Given the foregoing discussions of *r* loss and unaccented syllable loss, one might by now have the impression that Ocracoke pronunciations always involve the loss of sounds. But such is not the case. There are certain important brogue pronunciations that involve words with "extra" sounds—that is, sounds not present in these words in other dialects. In many instances, these "added" sounds are actually retentions of sounds that were present in earlier varieties of English but later were lost in most dialects. For example, in most English dialects, the *h* that we still see in the spelling of words like *honor* and *honest* actually used to be pronounced. There also was an *h* sound at the beginning of *it*. Similarly, *ain't* sometimes had an *h* in front of it as well, because one of the sources from which *ain't* derives is *haven't*. In most dialects, all traces of the initial *h* in *hit* and *hain't* have been lost, in spelling as well as speech. Not surprisingly, this *h* loss began in unaccented syllables and words, so that "She has *hit* in her house" became "She has *it* in her house" and "They *hain't* been there for awhile" became "They *ain't* been there for a while." In fact, this historic loss of the unaccented *h* is the same process by which today we get sentences like "I got *'im*" for "I got *him*."

Eventually, *h* began to be dropped from accented as well as unaccented positions, as in "When the winter set in, *it* set in" or "You *ain't* seen nothing yet!" In isolated dialects such as those in the mountains, on the islands, and in some rural southern areas, *h* was retained for a long while in stressed uses of *ain't* and *it*. Even today, we can still hear *hit* and *hain't* in the speech of older speakers in these areas, including Ocracoke.

Pronunciations like *hain't* for *ain't* are referred to as *relic forms*, because they are survivals from earlier periods of the English language. Relic forms tend to thrive in isolated areas, like Ocracoke before World War II, but they can rapidly disappear within a generation or two of exposure to outside dialects, unless the dialect speakers assign them some symbolic value. It does not appear that the initial *h* in *hit* and *hain't* has any special meaning for Ocracokers. In other words, *hain't* can't compare with *hoi toide*, which serves as a special marker of islander identity. Happily, though, at least *hain't* survives on the T-shirt given to us by Elizabeth Howard. For several years, this shirt was proudly displayed in the office of the North Carolina Language and Life project in Raleigh, North Carolina.

Sometimes, rather than retaining older sounds that other dialects have lost, a dialect may actually add new sounds. On Ocracoke, some words that have traditionally ended in an *-s* sound have an additional *-t* tacked onto them, so that we hear pronunciations like *once-t* (pronounced *wunst*) for *once*, *twice-t* for *twice*, *acrosst* for *across*, and *doast* for *dose*. Items like *once-t* and *twice-t* probably developed by analogy with words like *amidst*, *amongst*, and *against*, which already end in an *-st* sound in standard English. Changing the pronunciation of a word to make it sound more like a set of similar words is a common process in language evolution. *Once* and *twice* became *once-t* and *twice-t* quite some time ago, but only in some dialects. Among these dialects are a number of southern rural ones; this pronunciation is especially characteristic of southern Appalachia. *Acrosst*, found in a number of dialects of English, probably developed as a blend of *across* and *crossed* and first appeared in English several centuries ago.

It is difficult to say exactly where *doast* (which rhymes with *toast*) for *dose* comes from. As we saw in Chapter 2, *doast* has various meanings on Ocracoke, ranging from its specialized use for one particular illness, the flu ("I got a *doast* today"), to a more general reference to a large amount of just about anything, as in "James Barrie caught a *doast* of fish." Perhaps *doast* derives from one of the most common meanings of *dose*, to give out medicine, as in "The doctor will *dose* me up real good to help me feel better." When *dose* is used in this sense, it may be put into the past tense by adding an *-ed* ending, as in "The doctor *dosed* me up real good." Thus *dose* becomes *dosed*, which then becomes a word in its own right—*doast*. Although *doast* for *dose* is found in Appalachian as well as Ocracoke speech, we first noticed this pronunciation on Ocracoke, where people have occasion to talk about the range of meanings associated with *dose*, from sickness to a large catch of fish, on a regular basis.

PERSPECTIVE ON PRONUNCIATION

Although our description of some of the pronunciation features of Ocracoke English may have seemed a bit detailed to those who don't want to study dialects for a living, the important point is that these features—and those of all English dialects—are characterized by complex, rule-governed patterns. The overall impression of Ocracoke English that emerges from an examination of its pronunciation is that the Outer Banks brogue is distinctive, not because of the many structures found only in this dialect, but because of the way in which various pronunciation patterns have been joined together in the formation of this particular variety. For example, southern-sounding pronunciations like *feesh* and *fraysh* occur side by side with nonsouthern dialect features such as the pronunciation of the *r* in words like *car* and *farm*. When unique Outer Banks pronunciations like *hoi toide* and *saind* are factored in, the end result is a dialect quite unlike any other.

Ocracoke English also brings together British pronunciations from southwestern, midland, and even northern English dialect areas. It is virtually impossible to make direct, simple connections between individual British English dialects and the Ocracoke brogue, given the fact that Ocracoke's original settlers came from a number of different British dialect areas and intermingled with

Maurice Ballance relaxes on the "pizer" with his guitar. (Photograph by Ann Sebrell Ehringhaus)

other immigrants from all over the British Isles once they got to the colonies. Further, all languages and dialects change over time, and if there is little contact between two dialect areas, as with Britain and the young United States, these changes may take quite different directions in the two places. We all know how different British English and American English have become over the centuries since the two varieties first separated. Just imagine the differences among individual dialects of both languages that must have arisen in that time!

Our investigation of the Ocracoke brogue can teach us other lessons about how languages and dialects change. We know that individual features change at different rates and at different times. Some disappear within a generation or two, while others hold out against change; still others survive but are modified. Middle-aged Ocracokers may retain certain older pronunciations, such as *twice-t* for *twice*, while at the same time scorning other relic forms, such as *deef* for *deaf*, even though they may recall that older speakers on Ocracoke once used that pronunciation. In fact, *deef* can still be heard in other rural parts of the southern United States, as well as in northern and southwestern regions of England. Along with the traditional pronunciations that they have retained and those they have lost, Ocracokers have modified other older expressions. For example, whereas Ocracokers historically used to pronounce nearly all their *r*'s, many islanders now leave out a few *r*'s in words like *brothuh* and *agg'avate*, thus bringing their pronunciations a little more in line with those of their neighbors in the mainland South.

Social judgments about pronunciations can change as rapidly and arbitrarily as the pronunciations themselves. We have seen that the social significance of *r*-lessness has been particularly susceptible to change over the years, as one generation's elite pronunciation turns into the next generation's linguistic embarrassment and vice versa. Other pronunciation traits, too, have undergone the same fate. People are often surprised to learn that the pronunciation of *-ing* as *-in'* in words like *swimmin'* for *swimming* and *bakin'* for *baking* was once standard. In the earliest form of English, the *-ing* ending was pronounced just as it is spelled. It gradually came to be pronounced as *-in* in all classes of society, including the most elite. However, in the first quarter of the nineteenth century, people again began to consider *-ing* to be the "correct" form. This new pronunciation was adopted by the elite city-dwelling classes, while those who lived in more rural areas with limited access to cultural innovations were left behind.

Often, outsiders don't appreciate that speakers of Ocracoke English and other rural, isolated dialects who say *swimmin'* and *bakin'* are actually using forms that were once considered proper English. Instead, they simply judge such pronunciations on the basis of today's standards, not realizing that linguistic standards change readily over the course of history. Changes in dialect forms can come about in a variety of ways, but the bottom line as far as their social standing goes seems to be the same: the social status of a pronunciation comes from the status of the people who use it. We hope that a growing appreciation for the cultural heritage of Ocracoke will lead to a corresponding increase in respect for the traditions that have resulted in the brogue's distinctive pronunciations.

Saying a Word or Two

4

       The Ocracoke dialect consists of more than distinctive words and pronunciations. The essence of the brogue can be found in the way words are put together to form sentences as well. Consider the following passage, which comes from a story told by one of Ocracoke's best storytellers, Essie O'Neal, who was seventy-nine at the time of our interview with her. Essie O'Neal has led a colorful life, fishing side by side with island fishermen and raising eleven O'Neal sons over the years. She injects a lot of this color into every story she tells, as we see in this excerpt, which is set during one of the worst storms to ever hit Ocracoke, back in 1944. If you want to find out how this story ends, it appears in its entirety in Chapter 7, along with another of Essie O'Neal's engaging tales and several other island stories.

It come all the sudden. We had a pretty day, just like this. No wind, pretty sunshine. And the neighbor called that day and said, "There's a bad storm a-heading right straight for us." We didn't believe it. "There ain't no storm, there ain't no storm come."

She said, "Yes, it's headed right straight for Cape Hatteras."

It was a pretty, calm day; and that night, after it got to dark good, I went out with Harry, went out on the porch, and the stars was shining. He says, "I don't think there's no storm. It don't look like a storm." Everything was calm. But let me tell you, when we woke up the next morning, I thought the roof was gonna come off the house. I never heard such a hard wind—blowing a hundred miles. I never heard such a hard wind.

Harry said, "You better get up and get all them kids ready and get them dressed. We'll have to leave here."

I was working as fast as I could to get them all and put them to the table, give them breakfast and everything. Harry looked, and the tide was a-rolling right in the yard. It come up so fast; it was a-rolling in the yard. And that's when we left. When we left out of that gate, I tell you, it was about four foot of water in the gate when we left out. We had to leave there in a boat.

Much of the flavor of this story comes from the sentence structures, not from dialect pronunciations like *hoi toide* or dialect words like *meehonkey* or *quamished*. In just these few sentences, Essie O'Neal uses a good number of the Ocracoke structures we will discuss in this chapter. A classic one is the use of an *a-* (pronounced *uh*) in front of certain *-ing* words, as in "There's a bad storm *a-heading* right straight for us." Another one is *ain't*, as in "There *ain't* no storm." Yet a third dialect construction, the use of a double negative, occurs in the very same sentence. Essie also uses *to* for *at* in "I was working as fast as I could to get them all and put them *to* the table"—another marked feature of the Ocracoke brogue. Further, she uses the dialect plural *foot* for *feet* in "It was about four *foot* of water in the gate" as well as an Ocracoke subject-verb agreement pattern, which is shared with a number of other dialects, when she says "The stars *was* shining." Finally, we see *come* for *came* in "It *come* all the sudden" and "It *come* up so fast."

Sentence structures are a vital component of any distinctive dialect, including the Ocracoke brogue. Some of these structures are unique or practically unique to particular dialects, such as the use of *to* instead of *at*, as in "I put the children *to* the table." This dialect feature is found in only a few areas of the country, including Ocracoke and coastal areas to the north such as Tangier Island, Virginia, Smith Island, Maryland, and the Delmarva Peninsula. However, most sentence structures are shared among dialects. For example, the use of an *a-* with *-ing* verbs, a feature we call *a- prefixing*, is found in the Appalachian dialect area as well as among older Ocracokers. And certain other features, such as *ain't* and double negatives, occur frequently in dialects across America. Just as with the vocabulary and pronunciation, the distinctiveness of the Ocracoke brogue's sentence structure patterning has more to do with the particular *combination* of structures than with any one isolated characteristic found only on Ocracoke or the Outer Banks.

Speakers may be selective in which grammatical structures they include in their speech and which ones they leave out. The features used—and even how often and in what social situations they are used—depend on the speakers' ages, the people they associate with, and even whether they consider themselves true O'cockers or not. Many of the structures we consider integral parts of the traditional brogue are used mainly by older speakers, but there are a few middle-aged and even younger speakers who also employ some of these older constructions. Similarly, some older islanders don't use as many of the traditional brogue features as we might expect. For example, older Ocracokers like Essie O'Neal are usually the ones who attach the *a-* prefix to *-ing* verbs, particularly when telling stories. But some of the island's oldest storytellers rarely do this, whereas a few youngsters who aspire to storytelling fame frequently use forms like *a-hunting* and *a-running*.

Many of the Ocracoke sentence structures we describe are considered by some people to be "incorrect English" or "bad grammar." That is, sentences such as "There *ain't* no storm" may be viewed as reflections of ignorance or laziness on the part of speakers rather than as integral parts of a genuine dialect heritage. However, linguists who study sentence structure, which they refer to as *grammar*, know that speakers use the structures they do for valid reasons. Often, nonstandard sentence structures reflect older patterns that once were perfectly standard. For example, double negatives used to be well accepted in English; in fact, at one point in the history of English, there was no other way to form a negative sentence that made any sense. Similarly, subject-verb agreement patterns such as "The *stars was* shining" can be found in a number of older English dialects, including the Scots-Irish from which much of today's brogue derives.

Another reason speakers use so-called nonstandard sentence patterns is that sometimes these patterns are more linguistically "natural" than standard ones. In particular, it is very natural to unconsciously regularize any irregularities that occur in language patterns. For example, speakers often add the regular plural *-s* ending to irregular plural verb forms. Essie O'Neal does this in another of her stories when she uses *sheeps* for the plural of *sheep*. *Ain't* also represents a regularization, even though its use is considered by some to be the worst linguistic sin in English. The verb *to be* is highly irregular in standard English, and speakers have to memorize different forms for use with particular subjects: *I am, you are, she is, we are,* and *they are,* as well as the totally different forms *was* and *were* in the past tense. These same various forms must also be used in negative sentences: *I am not, you aren't, she isn't, we aren't,* and *they aren't.* In dialects that use *ain't,* one form suffices in all cases: *I ain't, you ain't, she ain't, we ain't, they ain't.* This form even works with *I.* There is no standard contraction of *am not,* as *amn't* is considered nonstandard in British English and isn't used at all in American English. Thus *ain't* helps repair a "gap" in the standard English system as well as regularizing the very irregular verb *to be.*

So why are nonstandard forms looked down on if they serve to "fix" problems with the standard English system and have a rich historical legacy? The reason is the same as the reason why some pronunciations are scorned. Certain forms are adopted by culturally and educationally elite groups and so become accepted, whereas other forms do not find favor with the "right" classes. And just as with pronunciation, the sentence structures that are considered standard may vary from region to region and change over time. A sentence such as "I *might could* go to the store" is hardly noticeable and almost standard in the American South; it is quite noticeable and nonstandard in the North. And even though double negatives may be considered quite unacceptable today, they were once standard enough for even Shakespeare and Chaucer, as we see in the following passage from the *Canterbury Tales*.

> He never yet no vileinye ne sayde
> In al his lyf, unto no maner wight.
> [In his whole life, he never yet has not spoken no rudeness to no sort of
>   person.]
> (General Prologue, ll. 70–71)

To make this chapter easier to read, we have classified the sentence components of Ocracoke English into three groups based on three major parts of speech: verbs, adverbs, and nouns, with the latter class including both nouns and pronouns. We have also included a section on how negative sentences are constructed on Ocracoke, because dialects often form negatives in ways that are noticeably different from standard negative constructions.

VERBS

Verbs play a large role in setting the various dialects of English apart from one another. The verb usages that we have found on Ocracoke help strengthen the connections we've already established between the brogue and other dialects that developed in isolated areas like Appalachia and Tangier and Smith Islands.

A- Prefixing

The attachment of an *a-* prefix to verbs that end in *-ing* is a well-known feature of American English dialects that have existed in relative isolation from other dialects. Constructions such as "He went *a-fishing*" or "The baby was just *a-hollering*" are also found in Ocracoke English, although their use is fading rapidly. Nonetheless, this *a-* prefix still crops up occasionally, mostly as a vestige of a once vibrant pattern for adding prefixes to certain kinds of words.

We can trace the *a-* prefix to a period in the history of the English language, several centuries ago, when such forms were widespread. Historically, the *a-* prefix developed from the words *at* and *on*, which used to precede *-ing* verbs in sentences such as "She is *at* working" or "He is *on* working" to indicate that the action described was taking place as the sentence was being uttered. The unaccented words *at* and *on* were later shortened to *a-* and then attached to the verb. Still later, the *a-* sound disappeared from many American dialects, but not from those spoken in isolated rural areas. The prefix is pronounced with an *uh* sound; and the *-ing* is always pronounced as *in*, in keeping with earlier practice. Nowadays, *a-* prefixing is not used in written communication, but letters from Ocracokers in the 1800s show that they did use it, spelling it with an *a* just as we do. For example, Elizabeth Howard generously shared with us a letter one of her island ancestors had written in 1886, in which we find the following sentence: "The boarders is *a gathering* up hear, and musquitos is stack up about two foot deep."

There are some dialects of English that continue to use not only the old *a-* prefix but occasionally even the full word *at* or *on* before *-ing* verbs. Thus "She's busy *at* working" may alternate with "She's busy *a-working*." Ocracokers, however, don't say *at* or *on* before *-ing* verbs, although they do still use the *a-* prefix, particularly in certain limited contexts—for example, when they want to emphasize a particular word or when they're telling an animated story. Even among the oldest speakers, the *a-* prefix is declining, though it sometimes appears where we least expect it. One of the youngest Ocracokers we talked to, a ten-year-old boy, uses it, although not very often and only when he's telling a story he's really excited about.

Even though the *a-* prefix is not standard English, it is governed by very specific usage rules. These rules are rarely written down; in fact, most people don't even realize they exist. Rather, they operate in the unconscious minds of speakers who use the form—and in the minds of quite a few who don't. For example, given the following sentence pair, can you tell, instinctively, where the *a-* prefix sounds "right" and where it sounds "wrong"?

A. James is a-fishing.
B. James likes a-fishing.

Chances are, even if you don't use the *a-* prefix yourself, you'll think sentence A sounds a lot better than sentence B. That's because one of the unconscious rules governing the use of the *a-* prefix is that it can only be attached to *-ing* words that act as verbs—that is, action words—as in sentence A. The *a-* prefix cannot be used with an *-ing* word that acts as a noun—that is, as the name of an activity—as in sentence B.

Other rules governing where *a-* prefixes can be used and where they can't involve certain pronunciation factors. For example, if the first syllable of the *-ing* verb is not an accented or stressed syllable, then it cannot take the *a-* form. If the first syllable is accented, then *a-* can be attached. Thus, "She was *a-hollering* at the dog" is acceptable; "She was *a-discovering* the cave" is not. The *a-* prefix is also more often attached to verbs that begin with consonants than to those that begin with vowels: "He was *a-chasing* the Russian Rat" sounds much better than "He was *a-eating* the ice cream."

In earlier forms of English, the *a-* prefix could be attached to certain other words besides *-ing* verbs. We still see remnants of this usage in "The building caught *a-fire*" and "They went *that a-way*." Sometimes even the full preposition is retained in such forms, as, for example, "The building caught *on fire*."

As noted, the use of the *a-* prefix is waning in Ocracoke English. Because we still hear it occasionally, however, we should recognize that it used to be a vital part of this language, and that it still serves a useful function as a marker of special emphasis or as a way of bringing stories to life.

Subject-Verb Agreement

The English language has a long history of marking verbs in some special way so that they match, or "agree," with the subject of the sentence. In modern English we use an -s or -es ending on most present-tense verbs to make them agree with third-person singular subjects (*She goes*), whereas other personal pronouns may take no ending at all (*I/you/we/they go*). In Old and Middle English, however, different endings were attached to present-tense verbs used with first, second, and third person subjects, and singulars and plurals were marked with their own endings as well. A comparison of the verb-agreement endings of a typical verb, *to go*, in Middle English and today's English shows the differences:

	MIDDLE ENGLISH		MODERN ENGLISH	
	singular	*plural*	*singular*	*plural*
1st person	go*e*	go or go*e(n)*	go	go
2d person	go*est*	go or go*e(n)*	go	go
3d person	go*eth*	go or go*e(n)*	go*es*	go

The complex subject-verb agreement system of Middle English eventually developed into the simpler system of Modern English. Today, the primary verb that doesn't follow this simpler pattern is *to be*, which as noted above has a number of different forms for different subjects and tenses: *am, is, are, was,* and *were*.

Our comparison of the agreement systems dominant in two different historical stages of English shows that these agreement patterns do not constitute inflexible, unbreakable rules. Instead, they change over time, often drastically. The "lack" of agreement we think we hear in certain dialects, particularly in historically isolated dialects like the Ocracoke brogue, reflects agreement patterns that used to be standard in earlier forms of English but are no longer considered acceptable. Although none of today's English dialects use the subject-verb agreement patterns of Middle English, many do retain a few traces of earlier ways of marking agreement.

For example, an -s ending is sometimes added to verbs used with third-person plural as well as third-person singular subjects, so that we may hear "people *goes*" instead of "people *go* or "The women *works* to the store." Ocracokers use this third-person plural *-s* ending, not because they don't know "proper" English, but because their form used to be a standard way of marking agreement with certain types of third-person plural subjects in older forms of English, including Scots-Irish English. These subject types are referred to as *collectives*.

Collectives are nouns that identify some sort of group or collection. They may be fairly specific, as in *government, group, family,* or *team*; or they may refer to more general collections of people or objects, as in *people, some of them,* or *a lot of them.* Because each of these words and phrases refers to one group composed of a number of members, there has always been a certain amount of confusion as to whether collective nouns should be treated as singular or plural. Some varieties, including standard English, classify them as plural and so use them with plural verbs, as in "people *go.*" Others classify them as singular and thus use them with verbs ending in *-s,* as in "people *goes.*" Neither agreement system can really claim to be the definitive, "correct" form. Remember that in standard British English, collectives like *government* are considered plural ("The government *were* debating"), but in standard American English many specific collective nouns are treated as singular ("The government *was* debating"). In older forms of English, general collectives like *people* were considered singular as well, so that a sentence such as "People *goes* to the store" would have been perfectly acceptable. This agreement system has been retained in a number of relic dialects in Britain and America, including Ocracoke English.

Verbs occurring with coordinate subjects may also have an *-s* on them. Coordinate subjects consist of two nouns joined by *and,* as in "The *boys and girls* played a game after school." In earlier forms of English, these could take singular rather than plural verbs—particularly when the second half of the coordinate subject was a singular word, as in "*Three boys and a girl is* coming over for dinner." This older agreement pattern is retained to some extent in Ocracoke English and in other dialects in historically isolated areas. Occasionally other plural subjects, such as *my friends* or *the old men,* may also take an *-s* verb, but this pattern is much rarer than the use of *-s* verbs with the special kinds of plural subjects discussed above.

Agreement with *To Be*

The verb *to be* is used far more frequently than other verbs, and it is also the only English verb that has so many different forms. There are therefore numerous agreement patterns for *to be* that differ from the agreement system now considered standard. In Ocracoke English, both present- and past-tense forms of *to be* show interesting agreement patterns. In fact, the Ocracoke past tense for *be* is nearly unique in American English. Notice how a young Ocracoker uses *weren't* in this excerpt from a ghost story: "I hearn some footsteps, and it *weren't* me and it *weren't* Linda. I heard some footsteps. It *weren't* the dogs, because the dogs was sitting near the beach by the water."

The standard English agreement pattern for past-tense *be* is irregular in that two different verb forms are used, *was* and *were*:

	Singular	Plural
1st person	I *was*	we *were*
2d person	you *were*	you *were*
3d person	s/he *was*	they *were*

A widespread tendency among English speakers is the attempt to regularize the verb *to be* by taking one form and using it for all subjects. In a number of American dialects, we hear *you was*, *we was*, and *they was* along with *I was* and *she was*.

In some British dialects, speakers use *were* rather than *was* for all subjects, resulting in *I were* and *she were* along with *you were*, *we were*, and *they were*. Even more common in British dialects is the use of *was* for all positive or affirmative sentences and *weren't* for all negative sentences. With this agreement pattern, we might hear "*They was* glad to be back home" along with "*I weren't* too happy about it." The entire pattern would look like this:

Affirmative		Negative	
I *was*	we *was*	I *weren't*	we *weren't*
you *was*	y'all *was*	you *weren't*	y'all *weren't*
s/he *was*	they *was*	s/he *weren't*	they *weren't*

Interestingly, Ocracoke English and other Outer Banks dialects are among the few in American English that use the above agreement pattern rather than just using *was* everywhere, in both positive and negative sentences. The young storyteller we quote above says *it weren't* and *the dogs was*. Even though the *was/weren't* agreement pattern isn't quite as regular as a *was/wasn't* system, it offers one big advantage over the simpler pattern in that it allows people to more easily distinguish between affirmative and negative meanings. *Was* and *wasn't* sound almost the same, except for the little -*n't* sound tacked onto the end of the latter. In rapid speech, this sound may be almost inaudible. But *was* sounds quite different from *weren't*, and so under the Ocracoke agreement system there is little chance of confusing positive and negative sentences.

There are other agreement systems that seem to be based on differentiating between affirmative and negative forms. For example, in mainland southern dialects, different vowel sounds separate the positive word *can* (pronounced to rhyme with *man*) from the negative *cain't*, which rhymes with *faint*. And in many dialects of English, including the Ocracoke brogue, the negative present-tense form of *to be* is *ain't*, rather than *isn't* or *aren't*. This form sounds nothing like the positive forms *am*, *is*, and *are*, and so it serves as a clear marker of negativity.

Another reason Ocracokers use the *was/weren't* agreement pattern is that forms like *it weren't me* and *he weren't here* are good markers of distinctive island speech. Like the *hoi toide* vowel, *weren't* seems to have acquired social meaning as an indicator of islander identity. We have noticed that O'cockers use *it weren't* more when talking with fellow islanders than when participating in a one-on-one interview with a member of our dingbatter research team. Further, when we directly ask people whether they say *wasn't* or *weren't*, they tell us they say *weren't*. Ordinarily, people tend to claim that they use standard forms, and therefore we expected Ocracokers to tell us they use *wasn't*, even if they really don't. The unexpected responses tell us that not only is *weren't* not considered "bad English" in Ocracoke, but it has a measure of positive value. Saying *it weren't* seems to be a way for islanders to let people know that they're Ocracokers—not mainland North Carolinians who tend to say *it wasn't*, *you wasn't*, and *they wasn't*.

Trudy Austin and Jana McLeod take a break on the dock.
(Photograph by Ann Sebrell Ehringhaus)

Special Helping Verbs

Helping verbs, or, more technically, *auxiliaries*, are words used with main verbs to add some special tense or tone to the meaning. For example, in standard English, the use of a form of *to be* with the verb *go* in "She *was going* home" modifies the meaning of the primary verb to indicate that an action was ongoing at some point in the past. All dialects of English share a common set of auxiliaries, but some dialects also have additional auxiliaries that add special nuances of meaning to the language. In a sense, these special auxiliaries show how nonstandard dialects can, at certain points, be more complex in their grammatical organization than dialects that are considered more standard. This complexity helps dispel the notion that nonstandard dialects are unworthy and less sophisticated approximations of the standard.

One of the special helping verbs found in Ocracoke English is referred to as *perfective* or *completive done*. In sentences such as "I *done forgot* to get the mail" or

"She *done took* the mail," *done* operates like an auxiliary rather than a main verb. In this use, it conveys the special meaning that the action has already been completed at the time the sentence is uttered. It has a meaning similar but not identical to the adverb *already*. In a related meaning, *done* used with the past tense of a verb may emphasize an action, so that a person who utters a sentence such as "She *done forgot* the mail" is stressing the fact that she unquestionably forgot the mail.

The use of *done* in Ocracoke English and other southern dialects, including Appalachian English, was apparently present in earlier stages of the language but has disappeared in most current varieties. Completive *done* was common during the Middle English period and persisted to some extent in northern England after the fifteenth century. Its use has been modified somewhat since that time, and it is now used more often for emphasis than to indicate simple completion of an action. On Ocracoke, completive *done* is not used as often as it is in some other isolated areas of the South, especially Appalachia, and it now seems most typical of the speech of middle-aged and older islanders.

Other special helping verbs in Ocracoke English are known as *modals*. Modals are words that refer to the speaker's mood or state of mind with respect to the action of the verb. For example, words like *can* (referring to 'capability'), *will* (referring to 'intention'), *may* (referring to 'permission'), and *should* (referring to 'obligation') are typical modals. On Ocracoke, as in much of mainland North Carolina, more than one modal may be used together, as in "I *might could* do it" or "They *might oughta* do it."

Most double modals consist of *may* or *might* coupled with *can* or *could*, but other combinations are possible; it is even possible to put three modals together, as in "She *might can should* do it." When the first word of a double modal is *may* or *might*, it seems to have about the same effect on meaning as it does when *might* is followed by a regular verb instead of another modal. For example, "I might could do it" means that I possibly am able to do something, not that I definitely am able to do it, just as "I *might* do it" means there's some doubt as to whether I'll really get the task accomplished. Even in those rare cases in which the first word of a double modal is not *may* or *might*, there is still some lessening of the intensity of the second modal.

Double modals can be traced to Scots-Irish English and to British dialects in northern England. They are also quite plentiful in today's Scots English. Although double modals are found in Ocracoke English, they do not occur as frequently as they do in most mainland North Carolina dialects. Their use is modest, more in line with their limited use in southern highland dialects such as Appalachian English.

Over time, certain helping verbs have begun to function in specialized, idiomatic ways. For example, *used to*, *must have*, and *like to have* now act more like single-word auxiliaries than like a verb plus *to* or *have*—that is, *useta*, *musta*, and *liketa*. These forms can even be used with modals and other auxiliaries in double-auxiliary constructions, as in "He useta couldn't do it" and "She musta didn't hear me."

The use of *liketa* even seems to have taken on special connotations related to the mood of the speaker. On one level, *liketa* may have a meaning similar to 'almost'. Thus, "She *liketa finished* digging the hole" means that she almost finished digging. Sometimes, though, speakers may use *liketa* to indicate that an action came very close to happening but didn't. We refer to this sort of situation as *counterfactual*. For example, if a speaker says, "I got so scared I liketa died," it means that in the speaker's opinion, the situation was such that she thought she might actually die, although of course she did not. Some dialects now only use *liketa* in this latter counterfactual sense, but Ocracoke English apparently is not one of them, because it retains the older, more literal meaning of 'almost' along with the counterfactual usage. When one Ocracoker told us that he didn't like the water much because one time "he liketa drowned," he was reporting a literal incident in which he almost did drown. The development of specialized uses like the counterfactual shows how the meanings of phrases and words can change over time in subtle but important ways. It also shows how dialect patterns can sometimes capture specialized meanings in ways that cannot be expressed as precisely by strictly following the rules of standard English.

Adverbs—that is, words that modify verbs—also differ from dialect to dialect. On Ocracoke, some adverbs have acquired special meanings not found in all varieties of English.

Positive *Anymore*

In English, the adverb *anymore* is commonly used in negative sentences such as "Rudy doesn't like fishing *anymore*," as well as in questions such as "Does Rudy go fishing anymore?" There are, however, some dialects in which this adverb may be used in positive or affirmative sentences like "Della likes watching videos anymore" to mean 'nowadays.' The implication is that Della did not particularly like to watch videos at a previous point in time, but now she does. Sometimes *anymore* is placed at the beginning of the sentence, as in "Anymore Della likes watching videos." Speakers of dialects that use so-called positive *anymore* take its use for granted, but speakers from other dialect areas find it rather unusual—and sometimes completely incomprehensible.

The use of positive *anymore* is noteworthy for a couple of reasons. First, it is generally considered a midwestern or southern highland feature, not a lowland southern one. In fact, this use of *anymore* strikes most southern lowland speakers as very odd indeed, unless they're from the Appalachian region, where we do find positive *anymore*. It is thus a striking example of a feature that separates Ocracoke English from the dialects of lowland North Carolina. Positive *anymore* is taken for granted in many areas of the United States extending from Pennsylvania through Ohio, Indiana, and points westward. It apparently can be traced to Scots-Irish ancestry, and it is still well attested in Northern Ireland. It is not, however, typically found in England. Thus, we see another instance in which some Scots-Irish features apparently were fused with structures from other parts of Great Britain in the formation of Ocracoke English.

Intensifiers

Ocracoke English, like much of mainland southern and Appalachian speech, includes expanded meanings of the word *right* that are not found in other dialects. In many American dialects, *right* is used as an adverb to intensify the meanings of adjectives that indicate location or direction in time or space. When someone says "She's right over there," *right* amplifies the meaning of *over there* by indicating that the subject of the sentence is located in one specific spot—not in a vaguely defined area. Similarly, in "He went right to the doctor," *right* intensifies *to the doctor* by indicating that the subject went to his destination immediately; he didn't drive down any side streets or run any errands along the way.

In Ocracoke English, *right* can be used as an intensifier with a wider range of adjectives. It is common to hear "David is right funny" or "It's right cold today." In this usage, *right* means 'very' or 'really'. *Right* can also be used in combination with a quantity word like *many* in sentences such as "He caught *right many* crabs today" or with *smart* in constructions such as "They lived there a *right smart* while." The intensifying use of *right* with adjectives and adverbs as found in Ocracoke and many southern varieties can be traced back at least to the fifteenth century; it occurs frequently, for example, in the writings of Shakespeare. The word's more limited usage as an intensifier of directional or locational adjectives, which we find in many northern American dialects, doesn't have nearly as long a history as the more general usage we still hear in Ocracoke, Appalachia, and other parts of the American South.

One intensifier we have found only on Ocracoke is the use of *some* with adjectives, as in *good-some* or *nasty-some*. If a person says "The meal was *good-some*," the food was extra special; but if a person says "It was *nasty-some*," you might want to avoid serving that dish again. When *-some* is attached to an adjective, it no longer acts as a separate word but as a part of the adjective. That is, *good-some* really counts as a single word, *goodsome*, just like the general English words *awesome* and *wholesome*. We know that *-some* words are inseparable; that is, nothing can come between an adjective and its *-some* ending. A person can't say "The food was *nasty* sitting in the dish *some*."

Several other patterns also govern how *-some* is used. First of all, *-some* can only attach to words of two syllables or less. People can say *nastysome* or *uglysome*, because *nasty* and *ugly* are two-syllable words. But they can't say *beautifulsome* or *differentsome*. Also, *-some* generally comes at the end of the sentence, as in "He was uglysome" or "The food was goodsome." It doesn't usually occur in the middle of a phrase, as in "He was an uglysome man" or "It was goodsome food." At first glance, this unusual Ocracoke use of *-some* just seems like a minor word difference, but further investigation shows that it is another example of the intricacy of dialects like Ocracoke English.

NOUNS AND PRONOUNS

Few, if any, of the Ocracoke dialect features associated with nouns and pronouns are unique to Ocracoke speech. Rather, it is the blend of particular constructions that sets Ocracoke apart as a dialect area.

Plurals

One feature of the Ocracoke dialect related to nouns has to do with how certain plurals are formed. In most varieties of English, almost all plurals are formed by adding an *-s* or *-es* to the noun, as in "Today I ran one *mile*, but yesterday I ran three *miles*." In Ocracoke English, the plural *-s/-es* may be absent, but only on certain types of nouns referred to as *weights and measures nouns*; these include words like *pound, gallon, inch, mile,* and *year*. The *-s* may be left off such a noun only when it is preceded by a word indicating quantity. That is, the absence of an *-s* is acceptable in phrases like "three hundred *pound* of flounder" and "It's three *mile* up the road," but not in a sentence like "Yesterday I drove for *mile and mile*." Because the weight noun *pound* is frequently used with reference to fishing, this is the word for which we are most likely to find plural *-s* absence when we talk to Ocracokers. However, the same construction applies with other measure nouns like *foot, inch,* and *mile*. The pattern of *-s* absence with nouns of weights and measures is common elsewhere in the American South and is also well documented in Irish English and in areas of England, particularly in the north.

Another unusual noun construction found among some Ocracoke English speakers is the regularization of noun plurals that are formed irregularly in socially preferred varieties of English—just as some irregular verb forms, such as *to be*, are also regularized. This regularization applies both to nouns that form their plurals in some way besides adding *-s* or *-es* and to those that do not have a plural form. For example, *oxen* may be regularized to *oxes* or *gentlemen* to *gentlemans*. Similarly, words like *aspirin* or *sheep*, which don't take an *-s* in their plural forms according to standard English rules, may become *aspirins* or *sheeps* in Ocracoke English. This type of regularization has been taking place for centuries now and is found in practically all dialects. The "adjustment" of irregular forms is a natural tendency for speakers of all languages and dialects, and one that often leads to permanent changes in even the standard version of a language. Because people who aspire to standard speech tend to shy away from "improper" forms like *oxes* or *foots*, however, it is the speakers of less socially elite dialects who tend to spark changes toward regularization.

Possessive Pronouns with *-N*

Most of the distinctive features relating to pronoun use in the Ocracoke brogue affect small sets of pronouns or individual pronouns within a limited set. One of the older pronoun forms, now rapidly vanishing, is the use of an *-n* ending on pronouns indicating possession, such as *yourn*, *hisn*, and *hern* for *your*, *his*, and *hers*. These forms are derived from *-en* forms that historically were scattered throughout various regions of England, including those that contributed heavily to Ocracoke English. The *-n* form has survived in the standard English possessive pronoun *mine* and, to a limited extent, in the now-archaic *thine*, as in "It is *thine*." Occasional uses of *yourn* or *hisn* by the oldest members of the Ocracoke speech community are retentions of older *-n* possessives that were once widespread in Appalachia and the Outer Banks. Such forms occur at the ends of sentences or phrases, as in "It is *hisn*" or "It was *yourn* that I took." They are not typically placed before nouns, as in "It was *hisn* book." This usage restriction parallels the one governing the use of *mine* in standard English, which is correct in "It is *mine*," but not in "It is *mine* book." (Of course, we do find archaic usages such as *mine eyes*, but today's English speakers would not tend to construct sentences with such forms.)

Plural *Y'all*

The case of the second-person plural pronoun in English is a classic example of how speakers unconsciously tend to smooth out irregularities and fix gaps in their language. Consider the set of standard English pronouns:

	Singular	*Plural*
1st person	I	we
2d person	you	you
3d person	he/she/it	they

In almost all cases, this set allows us to readily distinguish singular from plural subjects. The only problem is the *you* pronoun, which has the same form whether we're talking to one person or to a whole group. This lack of distinction can promote a lack of understanding. For example, suppose you are sitting in a crowded room and someone walks in and says, "I need to talk to you." You may be confused as to whether this person is about to address the entire room or about to take you aside and convey some personal information to you alone. Speakers of a number of American dialects have taken care of this potential comprehension problem by inventing second-person plural pronouns that sound different from the singular form. For example, in the lowland South, speakers often say *y'all* for plural *you*, whereas in certain other dialect areas, especially in the North, speakers may say *youse*, *you guys*, or even *you'ns* (short for *you ones*). In Ocracoke, speakers use the mainland southern word *y'all*.

One of the questions that puzzles linguists who study southern dialects is whether *y'all* can ever be used to refer to one person rather than to two or more people, as in "Chester, will *y'all* go to the store again?" On Ocracoke, it seems that *y'all* can only be used for more than one person, with one exception. Sometimes, as a kind of set phrase, *y'all* may be used to refer to a single person. For example, if you're the only one in the community store on Ocracoke, you might be addressed with the phrase, "Can I help y'all?" or, when you're leaving the store, with the farewell phrase, "Y'all have a good day now."

Negative sentences in the Ocracoke brogue are, for the most part, similar to negatives in other American dialects. Some of the features related to negation are well known because they serve as markers of nonstandard speech or "incorrect" English. For example, the negative word *ain't* is considered very bad English indeed, as is the use of so-called double negatives, in sentences such as "He *isn't* doing *nothing*." However, as with other sentence structure features, most nonstandard ways of forming negative sentences make perfect sense in terms of language patterning. And in fact, a number of nonstandard negative structures were once standard in earlier periods of English.

Double Negatives

We are all familiar with the "two negatives make a positive" rule, yet many dialect speakers continue to form sentences like "He isn't doing nothing." Why do so many people violate this rule of standard English? The answer is that this rule is a rule of logic or mathematics—not a language rule. Although two negatives do cancel each other out in certain math operations, in language they serve to reinforce each other. Using two or more negatives per sentence is standard in a number of the world's languages. For example, in standard Spanish, it is quite proper to say *"No hace nada,"* which translates literally as "He (or she) isn't doing nothing"; in fact, *"No hace algo,"* which translates into the perfectly good English sentence "He (or she) isn't doing anything," is blatantly wrong in Spanish.

Double or multiple negatives were also standard in earlier periods of English. The change from indicating negation in several places in a sentence to marking negation in only one place took place rather abruptly. Just a couple of centuries ago, a handful of authorities decided that language ought to work like math, even though it really doesn't, and so they instituted the "two negatives make a positive" rule. Since that time, multiple negation has been frowned upon in English. But despite the negative social value this construction has acquired, speakers continue to use it anyway because it's very natural linguistically and because it's a part of their language heritage as speakers of English.

Ain't There Other Negatives?

While the use of *ain't* is universally recognized as a stigmatized feature of American dialects, it has proven remarkably resistant to attempts to weed it out. *Ain't* is just as widespread in Ocracoke English as it is in other dialects. As we will see, the persistence of *ain't* is probably due to its useful language function.

In Ocracoke speech as well as other dialects, *ain't* is used in place of *am not*, *are not*, *is not*, and *have* (or *has*) *not*, as shown in the following examples:

am not	I *ain't* supposed to do it, am I?
are not	You *ain't* tired, are you?
is not	She *ain't* here today, is she?
have not	They *ain't* left yet, have they?

Ain't probably has several historical sources, including *am not*, which became *amn't* and later *ain't*. Another source is *are not*, which became *ain't* when *aren't* lost its *r* sound in some dialects (as in older southern American English and present British English), becoming *ahn't*, which later shifted to *ain't*. *Haven't* could also have become *ain't* through the loss of the *h* and *v* sounds from this word in rapid speech. Interestingly, the form *hain't*, in which the *h* has not yet been lost, still alternates with *ain't* among older speakers in some relic dialect areas, including Ocracoke.

There are a couple of good reasons why *ain't* is so persistent in the face of constant pressure to eliminate it. For one, it provides a negative word that sounds sufficiently different from the affirmative that the two can't possibly be confused. With a word such as *aren't*, the difference between "They *are* near us" and "They *aren't* near us" may be difficult to hear in natural, rapid conversation. *They are* and *they ain't*, however, are much easier to differentiate. *Ain't* is also an especially good choice as a negative form because it can be used with all subjects. In affirmative sentences, as well as in standard English negative sentences, we have to use different verb forms for different subjects: *am/am not, is/n't,* and *are/n't.*

No wonder, then, that *ain't* survives in Ocracoke and across America and Britain in the face of unrelenting social pressure to eliminate it. Though "correct" forms like *isn't* and *aren't* may hold sway in the realm of proper etiquette, nothing beats *ain't* in terms of linguistic naturalness and effective communication.

Other Negative Patterns

Other negative constructions in Ocracoke English may stand out to outsiders as well. For example, there is the occasional use of *nary* for *not any*, as in *"Nary a person talks like that."* Older brogue speakers are most likely to use this form, but middle-aged speakers occasionally do so as well, primarily for special effect but also when they're just talking naturally among friends.

Finally, there are some contractions that may strike outsiders as unusual, especially northerners. Contractions are shortened forms of certain kinds of words. For example, *I'll* is a contracted form of *I will* and *won't* is a contracted form of *will not.* These examples illustrate two main types of contractions in English, the contraction of helping verbs and the contraction of the negative word *not.* Although both types can occur, they can't occur together, so that in certain sentences a speaker has to choose whether to contract the negative or the helping verb. In sentences such as "I will not be there" or "I have not been there," most northern speakers would choose to contract the negative, saying "I *won't* be there" and "I *haven't* been there." But Ocracokers, following a pattern we've found in other parts of the South and in England as well, may choose to contract the helping verb instead of the negative, saying *"I'll* not be there" and *"I've* not been there." As one Ocracoker said after our discussion of a unique Outer Banks word, "You'll not find that in Webster." She was right, and she said it in a way that certainly drew our attention to it.

Believe it or not, we could go on in much more detail about negatives and the grammar of Ocracoke English. But our important points have been made: Grammatical constructions that don't conform to standard English structures are not necessarily "bad" or "incorrect." In fact, sometimes nonstandard language patterns display a greater degree of regularity than their standard counterparts. Further, grammatical structures in dialects like Ocracoke English are rich with dialect history. Today, these structures are an integral part of what makes each dialect of American English unique and colorful.

No Dialect Is an Island

5

Tourists aren't the only ones who talk about the curious resemblances of the Ocracoke brogue to other dialects. The similarities and differences between Ocracoke English and other varieties of the language are intriguing to professional dialectologists as well. Examining these parallels in detail can tell us a great deal about the settlement history of Ocracoke and the other dialects that may have influenced the brogue. It can also tell us about the ways in which islanders use their language to shape and project their identity as Ocracokers. In previous chapters, we have talked about connections between Ocracoke English and other dialects, including those in places as far away as England and Australia and as close as neighboring Outer Banks islands. We now focus more directly on the relationship of the Ocracoke brogue with other American English dialects.

If we were simply to look at each individual characteristic of Ocracoke English by itself, it would seem as if the Ocracoke brogue were a random collection of northern and southern U.S. dialect characteristics. Like northern dialects, the brogue is a variety in which *r*'s are pronounced after vowels in words like *car* and *court*. But the pronunciation of *fire* as *far* reminds us of neighboring lowland southern speech. And the use of *anymore* in affirmative sentences like "There sure is a lot of traffic anymore" is shared by dialects in more northern areas, such as those in Pennsylvania, Ohio, and Illinois. The combination of features that makes up the Ocracoke dialect appears even more haphazard if we extend our comparison to include varieties of British English. We have already seen that there are a number of similarities between the brogue and British dialects ranging from southwestern to extreme northern varieties. And we have also noted some Irish-English connections.

The theory that members of a dialect group simply pick and choose their speech features from an available menu of traits found in various other dialects with which they have had contact is sometimes referred to by dialectologists as the *cafeteria principle*. In general, though, linguists don't think too much of this principle, which implies that the development of a dialect is a completely random process. Ocracoke English may sometimes look like a patchwork-quilt dialect compared to the seemingly uniform texture of other dialects. But this hardly means that there is no method to the apparent madness in the selection of source dialects. Instead, we believe that the selection of features that go into the making of a dialect is guided by a set of social and language-related factors.

From their careful study of language evolution over the centuries, linguists have determined that there are general principles that guide the development of languages and dialects. Languages are also affected by the ways in which people relate to one another within their communities and across other social groups. Figuring out the historical, social, and linguistic factors that have worked together to shape the brogue can be frustrating at times, because these factors sometimes interact in extremely complicated ways. But every time we manage to put together a few more of the social and linguistic pieces of the dialect puzzle, we are fascinated once again by just how complex language systems are—and how amazing humans are in their inborn ability to learn and reshape languages.

In the following sections, we review some of the vocabulary, pronunciation, and sentence structures of the brogue in order to show how Ocracoke speech both resembles and differs from four other dialects of American English. First, we compare Ocracoke with other Outer Banks and Core Banks communities. So far, the island community we've studied in the most detail is Harkers Island, a Core Sound island to the south of Ocracoke. The Harkers Island community has a settlement history similar to that of Ocracoke and has also been isolated for most of its existence. We conducted about fifty interviews with native islanders ranging in age from ten through eighty-five to get a picture of this dialect across different generations. We also examined studies of the Outer Banks areas by other researchers to help us arrive at an overall picture of Banker speech.

Our second comparison is with the highland South or Appalachian English dialect. This dialect actually consists of a number of subvarieties, but a core of shared language features defines the dialect as a whole. It is concentrated in the mountainous areas of western North Carolina, eastern Tennessee, eastern Kentucky, West Virginia, southwest Virginia, and the highland areas of northern Georgia and Alabama. Over the past two decades, we have conducted interviews with more than two hundred speakers of all ages in some of the more remote, rural areas of these highlands. Our in-depth study of the speech we gathered there has helped us develop a detailed description of the general features of this dialect. In addition, we supplemented our own studies with a number of excellent dialect descriptions by other scholars of specific regions within this large dialect area.

The third area of our comparison is the lowland South. This area encompasses eastern North Carolina and eastern Virginia and extends to points southward into South Carolina, Georgia, and Alabama. We have used a number of currently available dialect studies to guide us in understanding these varieties.

Finally, our fourth area of comparison encompasses a rather vaguely defined dialect region that we call the non-South. This region extends from New England and the Northeast through the midwestern United States. Usually, we wouldn't lump together speakers from locations as obviously different as Boston, Philadelphia, and Chicago, but certain aspects of these dialects uniformly distinguish them from typical southern speech, so the general non-

South designation is a convenient one for our purposes here. Again, our main goal in this section is to explore how the Ocracoke brogue compares with some other dialects of American English.

THE VOCABULARY CONNECTION

It is especially difficult to compare the vocabularies of different dialects because of the number of words potentially involved. When there are so many items available for study, it's difficult to choose specific words for comparison. In addition, as we discussed in Chapter 2, it's hard to tell exactly what is meant by "knowing" a particular dialect vocabulary word. Word knowledge may range from the exclusive use of a single word by almost everybody in a certain population to the bare recognition of a word by a handful of people. In a region like Ocracoke, which has experienced rapid economic and social changes over the last half-decade, many different levels of word knowledge are especially evident.

Older Ocracokers, we have noted earlier, readily recall the days when they all played the island version of hide-and-seek and called it by a once-common island term, *meehonkey*. Middle-aged islanders know the term as well, but they may or may not have ever used the word in daily conversation. And island children have no idea what the word means, unless an older person has happened to tell them about it. A word like *dingbatter* reverses this pattern of age-related word knowledge. This word has come into use only in recent years as a replacement for the older generation's term for outsiders, *foreigner* or *stranger*. Middle-aged and younger speakers know and freely use *dingbatter*, but the oldest speakers may not have heard the word.

We have to take all of these factors into account in our comparison, and we have to recognize that we can't predict with certainty which groups of speakers will use which words under which circumstances. As a rule of thumb, we say that a vocabulary item is found in a dialect area if it is known and used by a segment of the population, even if it is not currently in widespread use. For example, words like *fladget* for 'piece' and *counterpane* for 'bedspread' were once fairly widespread on Ocracoke, and they are still considered island words even though we no longer hear islanders using them on an everyday basis.

Our comparison of dialect vocabularies is also limited in that we deal with only a relatively small set of words. If we were to compare the complete Ocracoke vocabulary with all vocabulary words in the Outer Banks, lowland South, and Appalachian dialects, we would be examining thousands of words. And the numbers would get much larger if we were to look beyond these areas. In fact, the *Dictionary of American Regional English*, the most authoritative source for dialect words we have in this country, lists 50,000 regional terms, and that's not even counting the Ocracoke expressions *meehonkey*, *call the mail over*, and *miserable'n the wind*. We submitted these terms and a few other new items to the dictionary staff, and they will appear in the next edition of the work.

An exhaustive comparison of vocabulary items is a daunting task that goes far beyond the scope of this book. Here we simply examine a few representative items to give you an idea of how the Ocracoke vocabulary compares to those of other dialect areas. Our analysis will cover several different kinds of relationships among these various dialects.

First, the Ocracoke brogue includes some words that we have not found elsewhere, even on other Outer Banks islands. This set of words is a very small one, numbering perhaps no more than a few dozen expressions and including terms for locations or geographic features such as *up the beach* meaning 'off the island to the north', *down the beach* meaning 'off the island to the south', and *the Ditch* meaning 'mouth of the harbor'. These Ocracoke-specific words also include terms for games and activities, such as *meehonkey* and *whoop and holler* for local versions of hide-and-seek, *call the mail over*, and *scud* for 'car ride'. Although the set of words that are unique to Ocracoke is very small, and some words may even be restricted to particular groups within the island community, they are important, and some of them are used frequently in everyday speech. *Going up the beach*, meaning 'going off the island to the north', is a common activity often mentioned in conversation. If listeners aren't thoroughly familiar with what this phrase means, they might confuse it with *going across the beach*, which simply means 'going to the seashore'—that is, going just up the street from Ocracoke Village rather than all the way off the island. Similarly, when an islander says *the mail is called over*, she means that the day's mail has been placed in the boxes in the post office. So even though they are relatively few, the unique vocabulary words of Ocracoke are critical to understanding and participating in the daily routines of island life.

Most dialect words on Ocracoke are shared with other Outer Banks communities and also with some of the coastal mainland areas immediately adjacent to the Outer Banks, from the eastern portion of Carteret County in the south to Currituck County in the north. This set of words includes items like *mommuck* for 'harass', *slick cam* for 'very smooth water', *dingbatter* for 'off-islander', *quamish* for 'upset stomach', *hard blow* for 'strong wind', and so forth. Some Outer Banks words show a regional distribution even within the Outer Banks. *Bankers* is an older term apparently used more in northern areas of the Outer Banks than in the southern islands. Similarly, *dingbatter* may not be used in all areas of the Outer Banks. For example, on Harkers Island, *dingbatter* alternates with the term *dit-dot*, which was once used more than *dingbatter*.

Despite this variation within the Banks themselves, a few Outer Banks words have acquired a symbolic significance in distinguishing *hoi toiders* from the rest of the world. This significance is not at all diminished by the fact that some of these distinguishing terms, particularly those that represent relic retentions from earlier periods of English, such as *mommuck* and *quamish*, are found in other isolated dialect areas as well, although often with slightly different meanings. For example, *mommuck* and *token* are used by the Lumbee Indians of Robeson County in the southeastern portion of the North Carolina mainland. And *quamished in the stomach* has been reported in some other relic dialect areas of the South.

The largest group of dialect vocabulary words on Ocracoke are shared with dialect areas throughout the South, including the Appalachian region and the lowland South. This list of common terms is quite extensive and includes many southern-sounding words, such as *y'all* for the plural 'you', *carry* meaning 'escort', *cut on/off* for 'turn on/off', *fixin'* to for 'intend to', *reckon* for 'suppose', and so forth. Along with this set of noticeably southern vocabulary words that are still in active use, we find on Ocracoke some other southern terms that are fading from use. Only older speakers know about such words as *pizer* 'porch', *sack* 'bag', and *skillet/spider* 'frying pan' — and even some of these don't use the terms anymore. Without a doubt, though, most of the prominent vocabulary items currently in use in Ocracoke are southern-sounding.

The brogue does include a few northern terms, but it is more noteworthy for its paucity of northern words, at least at this point in its history. The term *nor'easter* is found in New England and on other Outer Banks islands as well as on Ocracoke, partly because weather is so important to communities that make their living from the sea and partly because watermen who work the sea historically have traveled up and down the East Coast in the course of their work. *Waterman* is itself an eastern coastal term for a central figure in marine culture. It is found scattered up and down the eastern seacoast, particularly in the Chesapeake Bay area of Virginia and Maryland, but also on the New England coast. It is not nearly as common along the Outer Banks, but its popularity there seems to be growing. Terms like *piazza* (related to *pizer*), which means 'porch', and *spider* for 'frying pan' are found in eastern New England as well as in southern dialect areas, but this vocabulary connection has more to do with common historical sources for the dialects spoken in the two regions than with current contact between New England and the Outer Banks.

We do, however, suspect that a study of terms related specifically to the maritime cultures of the entire eastern seaboard would yield a long list of similar words across many dialect regions. This list would include nautical terms like *scuttle*, meaning 'a small opening in part of a ship', and words for fish and other marine life, such as *peeler crab* for 'a crab shedding its shell' and *jimmy* for 'male crab'. It would also include a number of weather terms. For example, words for common types of storms such as *nor'easter* are shared along the eastern seaboard up through New England. Similarly, *cam* for 'smooth water' is used on Tangier and Smith Islands in the Chesapeake Bay area. A thorough investigation of such specialized marine vocabulary, often referred to as *jargon*, would require a separate study. Unfortunately, that will have to be left to more skilled seafarers than these quamished, seasick writers.

Table 1 summarizes the vocabulary connections we have discussed here. A solid circle indicates that the term is current in the region, whereas an open circle indicates that the word is known in the region but is used by only a few speakers. Most of these expressions were covered in Chapter 2, but a few appear here for the first time.

This brief comparison of vocabulary words among different dialects shows

Ken Ballance pauses for a moment as he waits for the ferry. (Photograph by Ann Sebrell Ehringhaus)

that it is not the few expressions unique to Ocracoke or the Outer Banks that highlight the distinctiveness of Ocracoke speech, although popular accounts of the brogue tend to focus on these unique words. The bulk of the current Ocracoke vocabulary has a decidedly southern flavor to it, seasoned with some special Outer Banks terms and spiced up with a few words found only on the island. Although we do find a few northeastern influences on Ocracoke, particularly words derived from the maritime cultures along the eastern seaboard, there is little doubt that most of Ocracoke's vocabulary is predominantly southern.

Word	Ocracoke	Outer Banks	Highland South	Lowland South	Non-South
up the beach 'north of the island'	●				
Russian rat 'nutria'	●				
meehonkey 'island hide-and-seek'	●				
call the mail over 'deliver the mail'	●				
Ditch 'mouth of harbor'	●				
scud 'ride'	●				
dingbatter 'off-islander'	●	●			
mommuck 'harass'	●	●			
slick cam 'very smooth'	●	●			
hard blow 'strong wind'	●	●			
quamish 'upset stomach'	●	●			
carry 'escort'	●	●	●	●	
fixin' to 'intendin' to'	●	●	●	●	
sack 'paper bag'	○	●	●	●	
y'all 'plural you'	●	●	●	●	
skeeter hawk 'dragonfly', 'crane fly'	●	●	○	○	
cut off/on 'turn off/on'	●	●	●	●	
reckon 'believe, imagine'	●	●	●	●	
tote 'carry'	●	●	●	●	
pizer 'porch'	○	○	○		○
skillet 'frying pan'	○	○	●	●	○
nor'easter 'storm from the northeast'	●	●			●

Very few of the sounds of Ocracoke are restricted only to the island or even to the Outer Banks as a whole. Even the well-known *oy* of *hoi toide* and the *ay* of *saind* ('sound') can be found in other regions. We have already discussed the British English dialect areas that share pronunciations with Ocracoke, but there are many similarities also with dialect areas in the U.S. For example, vowel sounds similar to the *hoi toide* and *saind* pronunciations have been noted on Smith and Tangier Islands in the Chesapeake Bay area. In addition, a series of interviews we conducted recently among older Lumbee Indians in Robeson County, North Carolina, uncovered the *hoi toide* pronunciation there as well. Our finding indicates that we cannot consider this pronunciation an exclusive Outer Banks sound, despite its association with the stereotypical brogue. At the same time, the shared *hoi toide* pronunciation suggests the fascinating possibility of a historic connection between Outer Bankers and the Lumbee Indians. The origins of the Lumbee are uncertain, and their native language was lost long before the majority of European settlers arrived in North Carolina. Perhaps establishing a connection to early Outer Bankers will help restore some of the group's lost heritage.

Interestingly, we did not find the *hoi toide* vowel in our previous surveys of Appalachian English, even though this dialect is very similar to the brogue in many ways. Of course, there are many places in Appalachia that we did not reach in our surveys. We also learned long ago never to be too insistent in our claims for the uniqueness of dialect features. Every time we maintain that a particular dialect feature is found only in one particular area, it seems to crop up somewhere else just to keep us humble.

Along with its classic *hoi toider* vowels, Ocracoke speech boasts a distinctive mix of northern and southern vowels, with the overall impression being southern. The *ee* vowel of *feesh* for 'fish', the *ay* sound of *fraysh* for 'fresh', and the *oo* sound of *poosh* for 'push' are prominent in today's southern American English as well as in the Ocracoke brogue, and they are becoming even more widespread. Similar pronunciations, however, are also present in the southwest of England.

Apparently these Old World sounds have been around for quite a while, so we cannot simply assume that Ocracoke adopted them from the southern U.S. mainland after most settlers had arrived in the New World. And what is perhaps the most stereotypical and widespread southern vowel pronunciation of all, the identical pronunciation of the different vowels in word pairs like *pin* and *pen* and *him* and *hem*, has been a noticeable trait on Ocracoke for some time.

Mixed in with general southern vowels on Ocracoke are several that are clearly nonsouthern, even if they don't necessarily sound distinctly northern. Although they are surrounded by the southern *hah tahd* vowel, a number of Ocracokers still say *hoi toide* to assert their identity as islanders. And although the younger generation may not use the traditional island pronunciation as often as their older relatives, they're not picking up the southern *ah* either. Perhaps this is the Ocracokers' way of saying "enough is enough" with respect to the southern pronunciation features they've allowed into their dialect over the centuries.

Islanders fully recognize that the southern *ah* for *i* is a mainland pronunciation, not an island one. We saw this with striking clarity when we were teaching a group of eighth-grade Ocracokers about the patterns of the brogue. As the students listened to a tape-recorded story told by a southerner who used the *ah* pronunciation in words like *raht tahm* for 'right time', they laughed, mimicked the strange pronunciation, and noted, "That pronunciation sounds like Raleigh!" A lot of lessons about language and social identity can be gleaned from an episode like this. The bottom line, though, is that the right time for the *raht tahm* pronunciation has not yet come in Ocracoke, and it isn't likely to arrive any time soon.

The vowel Ocracokers use in words like *bought* and *ball* is also distinctly nonsouthern and even sounds northern at times. Sometimes it sounds very close to the vowel in *put*, so that *ball* sounds almost like *bull*. This pronunciation is more similar to that of such northeastern cities as Philadelphia and New York than to the southern mainland pronunciation. In fact, we once played a tape of some Outer Bankers saying *bought* and *ball* for a group of people in Raleigh and asked our listeners to guess where the speakers were from. Most guessed that they were from the New York area rather than from North Carolina. In reality, however, this pronunciation of the vowel in *bought* and *ball* is most similar to British English and is one of the sounds that really serves to strengthen the Great Britain—Ocracoke connection.

About fifty years ago, one of the most distinctive sounds of the lowland South was the pronunciation of the *r* in *park* the *car*. In fact, the difference in this one sound between the mainland and the islands was once enough to make visitors feel that they had journeyed completely out of the lowland South during the boat trip to Ocracoke. But more and more mainland southerners in lowland regions have begun pronouncing their *r*'s as time goes by, and today we can no longer hear quite as sharp a contrast between the mainland and island *r*'s. But some of this historical contrast is still evident when we compare the speech of older lowland southerners on the mainland with that of older O'cockers.

A number of vowel pronunciations on Ocracoke suggest closer connections with sounds from the Piedmont and mountain regions of North Carolina than with the Coastal Plains area in the eastern part of the state. For example, the pronunciation of *bear*, *hair*, and *there* as *bar*, *har*, and *thar* is more like mountain speech than it is like the lowland South. In fact, this pronunciation is so strongly associated with the Appalachian dialect that it even surfaces in songs about the mountains. For example, "The Ballad of Davey Crockett" asserts that its hero "kilt him a *bar* when he was only three." To our knowledge, the famous Tennessee-born mountaineer never visited the Outer Banks, and if he had, he would more likely have kilt him a flounder or two rather than a mainland-dwelling *bar*.

Other prominent Ocracoke pronunciations such as *fraysh feesh*, the identical sound of *pin* and *pen*, and the retention of *r* following a vowel are as widespread in southern highland areas as they are in the lowland South. The way Ocracokers sometimes pronounce unaccented syllables is also reminiscent of some well-known Appalachian sounds, although these can be found too in rural areas of the lowland South. For example, in both regions, syllables can be dropped from the beginning and middle of words, as in *skeeters*, *taters*, and *sec'tary*. We also hear identical changes in final syllables, such as *-oh* becoming *-er* (in *feller* and *yeller*), and final *-a* (pronounced *uh*) becoming *-ee* (in *sody* and *extry*). An even closer match between the Outer Banks and Appalachia surfaces in the various consonant pronunciations that unite these areas, including the retention of the *h* in *hit* and *hain't* and the pronunciation of a *t* in words like *once-t* and *twice-t*.

A summary of similarities and differences in pronunciation between Ocracoke English and other dialects is given in Table 2. Although this comparison shows that many pronunciations of the Ocracoke brogue are identical to those of Outer Banks dialects, there are a few differences among the islands. For example, older residents of Harkers Island may substitute a *w* for a *v* in words such as *aggawaited* for *aggravated* or *wessel* for *vessel*, and there may be some fine-grained pronunciation differences among Outer Bankers even in the famous *hoi toide* vowel. However, the major pronunciation features certainly sound similar to the outsider. Islanders may be able to detect some of the small variances in pronunciation from island to island, but most mainlanders can't tell an Ocracoker from a resident of Harkers Island, much to the dismay of these communities.

Perhaps the most noteworthy aspect of Outer Banks pronunciations is their similarity to the patterns we find in Appalachian dialects. Almost all the pronunciation features of the brogue—except the classic *oy* and *ay* sounds in *hoi toide* and *saind*—remind us of Appalachian speech. There are probably a couple of reasons for this. First, early settlers to both regions came from some of the same dialect areas of England and Ireland. Second, and more important, both dialects developed in relative isolation from other American dialect areas. People in isolated regions often retain older speech traits while more mainstream dialects alter the older forms. Pronunciations such as *hit* for *it*, *bar* for *bear*, and the *r* in *park* apparently were standard and widespread throughout much of colonial America, from Philadelphia to Jamestown. These features eventually were changed in most of this area, remaining in only a few isolated pockets such as Ocracoke and Appalachia. The affinity between the mountain and island dialects of North Carolina shows how similar historical, social, and cultural influences, particularly isolation from the mainstream, may preserve the common linguistic heritage of two or more dialect areas even after centuries of separation.

Sound	Ocracoke	Outer Banks	Highland South	Lowland South	Non-South
oy (*hoi toide*)	●	●			
ay (*saind* for *sound*)	●	●			
h (*hit* and *hain't*)	○	●	●		
a (*bar* for *bear*)	●	●	●		
t (*once-t* and *twice-t*)	●	●	●		
ar (*far* and *tar* for *fire* and *tire*)	●	●	●	○	
unaccented syllable loss (*skeeters, agg'vate*)	●	●	●	○	
final *er* (*feller, skeeter*)	●	●	●	○	
pin (for both *pin* and *pen*)	●	●	●	●	
ee (*feesh* for *fish*)	●	●	●	●	
ay (*fraysh* for *fresh*)	○	●	●	●	
aw in *caught* (*u* of *put*)	●	●			●
loss of *r* (in *park* and *car*)				●	○

SENTENCE COMPARISONS AND CONTRASTS

In terms of sentence structure, the Ocracoke dialect is more similar to Appalachian English than to the English of the lowland South. Of course, the brogue does share some sentence constructions with the lowland South as well as with nonsouthern dialect areas. We have found virtually no substantial differences among Outer Banks communities with respect to sentence structure, unless we consider features such as the use of -*some* with certain adjectives, as in *goodsome, nastysome*, and *windysome*. This feature is well established on Ocracoke, but we haven't yet found it on other Outer Banks islands. Interestingly, the -*some* ending is found on Smith Island, Maryland, located to the north of Ocracoke in the Chesapeake Bay. However, here its usage is opposite that of Ocracoke -*some*, and a word like *goodsome* actually means 'somewhat good' rather than 'very good'.

Two features of Outer Banks sentence structure stand out because they are practically unique to the islands, at least among American English dialects: the use of *weren't* in sentences like "It *weren't* me" and the use of *to* for *at*, as in "She's *to* the beach." Saying "it weren't me" may be common in British dialects, but it is relatively rare in America. We find this construction in only a few isolated relic areas, and it doesn't occur very often even in the handful of dialects where we do find it. A few cases of "it weren't me" have been noted in Appalachia and also in our studies of Lumbee English. Parallels like this and the *hoi toide* pronunciation found in both the brogue and Lumbee speech strengthen the case for a Lumbee Indian–Outer Banks historical connection. We're still a long way from endorsing one of the popular theories regarding the origins of the Lumbee: that they are descended from the vanished Lost Colony, which included Virginia Dare among its members. But the linguistic links between today's Ocrackers and Lumbee Indians certainly suggest that there is some connection between the two groups.

Major sentence structures of Ocracoke English that are also important features of Appalachian English include the use of *a-* before verbs as in "I was *a-fishing*," verb agreement patterns like "*People goes* fishing," and the absence of a final -*s* on plural nouns referring to weights and measures, as in *two pound* or *three mile*. These constructions are present to a lesser degree in other rural southern dialects, including that of the Lumbee.

We also find in Ocracoke a number of general southern sentence structures, such as *might could* in "She *might could* do it," *done* in "The young'uns *done took* the skiff," and *liketa* in "I *liketa* drowned." The use of *anymore* in affirmative sen-

Natalie Schilling-Estes listens intently to island conversation. (Photograph by Herman Lankford)

tences such as "We watch a lot of movies *anymore*" is particularly noteworthy because it is so rare in the lowland South, instead being confined largely to the mid-Atlantic states and the midland U.S. However, we also find the construction in Appalachia, which again shows us that the mountains and the islands of North Carolina are united by strong dialect ties.

Table 3 summarizes some of the similarities and differences in sentence structure among Ocracoke English and other U.S. varieties. In many ways, this table looks much like the pronunciation table in its patterning. With the possible exception of the use of -*some* with adjectives, there are no significant differences between the sentence structures of Ocracoke and those of other Outer Banks communities. Different communities might use one particular trait to a greater

TABLE THREE: Sentence-Structure Relationships among Ocracoke English and Other Dialects

Structure	Ocracoke	Outer Banks	Highland South	Lowland South	Non-South
some with adjectives ("It's *nastysome*")	●				
weren't ("It *weren't* me")	●	●			
to ("She's *to* the store")	●	●			
a-prefixing ("He was *a-fishing*")	●	●	●	○	
-s absence (*twenty pound*)	●	●	●	○	
subject-verb agreement ("*People gets* upset")	●	●	●	○	
done ("She *done* messed up")	●	●	●	●	
double modals ("He *might could* come")	●	●	●	●	
right ("He's *right* silly")	●	●	●	●	
anymore ("We watch TV *anymore*")	●	●	●		●
multiple negatives ("*Nobody don't* like *nothing*")	●	●	●	●	●

or lesser degree. For example, the use of *weren't* in sentences like "I *weren't* there" seems to be more frequent among some middle-aged and younger speakers on Ocracoke than it is on Harkers Island, but the pattern nonetheless does occur in other Outer Banks communities such as Harkers Island, Salter Path, Hatteras, and Wanchese. Conversely, *a*-prefixing, as in "The sun is *a-shining*," shows less sign of fading from use on Harkers Island than on Ocracoke, as do some other significant Outer Banks features. Despite such differences, though, almost all of the sentence constructions on Ocracoke are also common to the Outer Banks as a whole.

Certainly there are ties, in terms of sentence structure, between the brogue and the lowland South, but the island-mountain connection is stronger. Virtually all of the prominent sentence structure features that separate Ocracoke English from lowland southern English, with the notable exception of the use of *weren't*, are characteristics we have also found in our surveys of Appalachian dialects.

THE OVERALL PICTURE

Although the sentence structure and pronunciation comparisons we have just made show parallel patterning, we have seen that vocabulary words align themselves differently across dialects. Whereas the sentence structures and pronunciations of the brogue show the strongest ties with Appalachian English, the Ocracoke vocabulary is most strongly related to that of the lowland South. Map 5 summarizes the overall relationship of Ocracoke English to other dialects when all three levels of language are taken into account. The darker the shading, the closer the relationship of the dialect to the Ocracoke brogue.

We suspect that the historical connections that unite the Ocracoke brogue with other isolated dialects such as Appalachian English will grow more obscure as the island continues to come into more and more contact with outside dialect areas. Although Ocracokers maintain great pride in their island heritage in the face of increasing contact with mainlanders, the fact is that their distinctive brogue simply isn't as strong as it used to be. Most O'cockers still use one or two features of the traditional brogue, such as *it weren't me* and the *hoi toide*

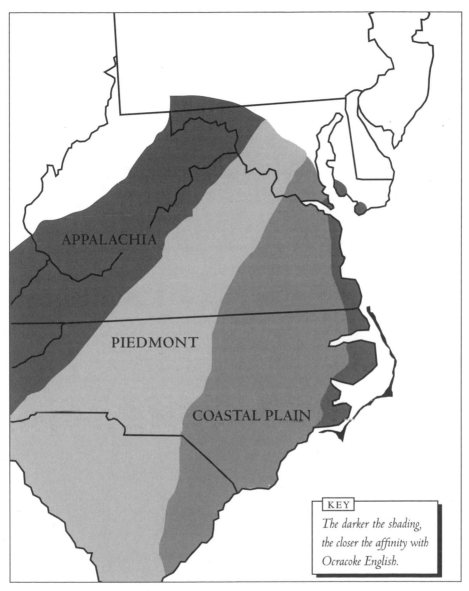

Map 5. Relationship of Ocracoke English to Other Dialects
(Map drawn by Shelley Gruendler)

vowel, to assert their islander identity, but nowadays they tend to find other ways of letting people know that they're islanders rather than mainland southerners. Today a person's Ocracoke heritage is a far stronger marker of islander identity than the brogue; the true mark of a genuine O'cocker is being from the right family, not speaking the right way. In the following chapter, we examine the fate of the fading brogue at greater length.

Ebb Tide for Hoi Toide?

6

Like most tourist sites, Ocracoke is well known for its T-shirts. The pictures and slogans on these shirts run the creative gamut—from a traditional shot of the historic Ocracoke lighthouse inscribed with the simple place name "Ocracoke, NC," to a sketch of an enormous island skeeter proclaiming, "Send more tourists, the last batch was delicious." Several years ago, we introduced yet another T-shirt with the slogan "Save the Brogue." On the back of the shirt, we listed some distinctive Ocracoke words and sayings—*mommuck, dingbatter, buck, call the mail over, miserable'n the wind,* and so forth. The shirt was our way of calling attention to the fact that the traditional brogue has been eroding rapidly and that this should be a matter of concern. In fact, we consider the brogue an *endangered dialect.*

In the biological sciences, the classification of species as endangered is a widely recognized and often politically charged act. Legislative action now protects a wide range of animals and plants on the brink of extinction, thanks to the combined efforts of concerned scientists and citizens. At the same time, the dramatic decline of the world's languages goes largely unnoticed, except by the affected speakers and a small group of linguists and anthropologists.

Compare the state of the world's languages with the condition of earth's mammals and birds. There are an estimated six thousand languages in the world, but the majority of these are rapidly heading toward extinction. At the current rate of language loss, somewhere between 50 and 90 percent of these languages will die out within the next century. In California alone, approximately twenty-five different Native American languages have lost their last speaker in the past century. And these were distinct languages, not mere dialects of the same language. By contrast, biologists estimate that less than 8 percent of all mammals and less than 3 percent of birds are imperiled. Furthermore, most of these species are classified only as threatened, not endangered. Clearly, there is an endangered-language epidemic under way.

Is the death of a language really comparable to the extinction of a biological species? Should we worry about language death as we do the death of animals? After all, people certainly don't give up talking when a language dies. They just use another language. In fact, the potential reduction of the world's languages to a few exclusive survivors may even be praised in some circles. From the standpoint of efficiency, international communication would be much easier if we all spoke the same language. This may be true, but there are other considerations. It is also true that it would be more efficient and economical if we all wore the same kind and size of clothing, but such lack of diversity wouldn't leave much room for the expression of individual or cultural identity.

A window of scientific opportunity closes when a language dies. The more languages there are, the more information we have about how language in general works, just as we learn more about the general nature of life from biological diversity. For example, the observation of many different kinds of birds can teach us more about the aerodynamics of flight than the observation of a single species limited to one size, weight, and skeletal structure. In a similar way, we can learn a lot more about the general nature of language by observing a host of languages than we can by observing only one or a few languages.

But there's more. When a language dies, an essential and unique part of a human culture dies with it. To imagine the personal impact, consider what it would be like to be the last speaker of a language with no one to talk to in your native tongue—the language of your childhood experience and your most fundamental emotional, artistic, and spiritual expression. That scenario might seem unimaginable for English speakers at this point, but it wasn't always so. English was once a minority language in danger of being overwhelmed by other languages, just like so many others now threatened with extinction.

It is understandable that linguists and anthropologists feel a deep sense of urgency about the threatened and endangered state of so many of the world's languages. But what about the varied dialects of one particular language? Linguists worry about the plight of minority languages worldwide, but even the most conscientious tend to overlook the threat to endangered dialects of "safe" languages. An endangered dialect is a unique variety of a language, spoken by a small number of people and threatened by encroaching dialects of the same language, much as the Ocracoke brogue is threatened by encroaching mainland dialects such as southern American English.

People may think that the death of a dialect is not nearly as significant as the death of an entire language, but this is not necessarily the case. For certain scientific purposes, it is just as important to study different dialects as it is to study different languages, because dialect studies show us how much variation languages can contain within themselves. Even if we're not interested in the scientific study of language, we should consider the toll a dialect's death takes on the humans who once spoke it. Saying that dialect loss is not as important as language loss is like saying that we should be vitally concerned with the preservation of the general species *canis familiaris*, or dogs, but not worried about particular breeds of dogs. After all, dogs come in so many breeds and can be mixed in so many different ways that the preservation of a particular breed may not seem very important. But suppose your choice in dogs were reduced to Great Danes when your favorite dog—and the only kind you had ever had in your home—was a miniature Pekinese? Ironically, at the same time that English is expanding as a world language and new dialects, such as certain kinds of Asian and African English, are being created, some of the most distinct dialects of English have been quietly vanishing. We consider the traditional Ocracoke brogue to be one of these threatened dialects.

THE ENDANGERED OCRACOKE BROGUE

A classic set of circumstances typically lead to a language's endangered status, and most of these circumstances are found on Ocracoke. Usually, social and historical conditions combine to threaten the established stability of a community and, along with it, the traditional language. For two and a half centuries, Ocracoke was isolated geographically, economically, and socially. The implementation of a state-run ferry service in the 1940s and a state highway in the 1950s allowed far greater access to Ocracoke than had been available before World War II, when boat transportation was sporadic and land travel took place over bare sand. With improved transportation, Ocracoke began to host ever increasing numbers of tourists and to acquire new residents from the mainland. The traditional Ocracoke brogue became a minority dialect on the very island that had nurtured and protected it for so long.

Today less than half the year-round population of six hundred are native O'cockers, and even fewer regularly speak the brogue. On some days during the summer tourist season, less than one-tenth of the people on the island are O'cockers. Due to the large number of tourists, the island economy has changed from one largely independent of mainlanders to one almost wholly dependent on outside money. The breakdown of economic and geographic barriers separating Ocracoke from the mainland has led to a corresponding breakdown in social barriers. Marriage outside the island community is becoming increasingly common. And the youngest islanders now interact on a daily basis with classmates, friends, and teachers whose families are transplanted mainlanders—and all of whom speak dingbatter dialects.

When social and historical circumstances dramatically change a community and an isolated language or dialect becomes a minority language in its native habitat, it becomes highly vulnerable. The very tourists and new residents who bring much-needed money to the island also pose a real threat to the traditional Ocracoke way of life. Ocracokers have lost even the privacy of their own homes as tourists wander through their backyards on a daily basis. Furthermore, tourism dollars have brought increased property taxes for all Ocracoke residents, whether or not they directly benefit from the tourist trade. Residents who could afford to pay the property taxes of the 1970s may no longer be able to afford them—especially some of the older people, now living on fixed incomes, who have been the stalwarts of the traditional culture. Values have changed, traditions have vanished, and outsiders have become more and more prevalent.

The threat to the Ocracoke brogue is very real. Once common dialect features are vanishing rapidly. If we compare just three generations within the same family, we can see how quickly a unique language can die. In some families, the grandparents may still retain many traditional speech characteristics, including the *hoi toide* vowel and the pronunciation of *sound* as *saind*. They may also use *a-* before *-ing* verbs, as in "She was *a-fishing*," and drop the *-s* after *pound* in *twenty pound*. Middle-aged speakers may or may not use these traditional pronunciations and constructions, and younger speakers will most likely avoid them.

Also within the same family, we may find older members who use traditional dialect expressions such as *token of death* for 'sign of impending death' or *fladget* for 'piece' living side by side with adolescents who have never heard these words at all. Young O'cockers are surprised when they ask their grandparents about older words and discover that many terms they are hearing for the first time were once in common use. Some traditional dialect items are disappearing a lot faster than the eroding Carolina beaches.

A language can die completely within just three generations, once the process begins. The first generation speaks the language fluently; the next generation speaks it haltingly; the third generation barely speaks it at all. Ocrakers born before World War II may be pretty well immune to losing their brogue, but young speakers who learned their dialect in the 1980s are a different story. Within forty years, the traditional brogue has fallen from its position as the majority dialect on the island into what we call moribund status. The term *moribund* is used to refer to any language that is no longer learned by children as their first language. Two generations ago, an Ocracoker who didn't speak the brogue was an oddity; today, the youngster who knows it is the exception.

When a language or dialect is moribund, its death is imminent—unless a dramatic reversal takes place.

As a dialect erodes, speakers use it in fewer and fewer settings. Further, when they do use a dying dialect, they tend to focus on how it sounds rather than on what they're talking about. They may also start performing for people who want to hear their "quaint" or "old-fashioned" speech, instead of using the dialect for real-life, everyday communication.

On Ocracoke, school-aged children may use some features of the brogue when talking informally with their friends, but they tend to speak differently in the classroom. Even among middle-aged speakers, the brogue is noticeably thicker when a group of islanders gets together for some traditional activity, such as playing poker or shucking oysters, than it is in other situations, such as conducting business with tourists in local stores. Some poker players even claim that fellow islanders have trouble understanding them during especially heated games, even though they are quite understandable at other times.

Some of the younger and middle-aged Ocracokers, particularly some of the men, are very much aware of the dialect and its diminishing role. These people grew up during the first wave of increased outside influence on the island. They are proud of the traditional Ocracoke brogue, and they lament its passing, often remarking that the brogue is fading among younger speakers. They are also well aware that their speech is an object of curiosity to outsiders, and they tend to exaggerate its more noticeable features, especially the well-known *hoi toide* pronunciation. It is, in fact, hard for islanders not to focus on the brogue when dingbatters are constantly demonstrating their stereotypical expectations of island speech. For example, we heard the following story from Candy Gaskill, a well-known O'cocker who manages Albert Styron's General Store, which is owned by her father:

> I had a lady in here last week I had a battle with. You might as well say a battle with, because she come up to the counter, and she said, "Speak!"
> I said, "Excuse me?"
> "She said, 'Speak!'
> "I was like, 'Do I get a biscuit?'"

She said, "I wanna hear you talk."

I was like, "I'm talking to you, ma'am."

And she was like, "No you're not, you're not talking right."

I said, "I've lived here, soon-to-be twenty-nine years in May," and I said, "I've talked this way all my life as far as I know." And I said, "I can't change it."

She's like, "Well, you're not talking the way you should be talking."

And I was like, "How should I be talking?" She said, "Well, you just don't have that accent."

And I said, "Well, I'm sorry."

Candy Gaskill's speech shows an interesting combination of things traditionally Ocracoke and importations from the mainland. For example, she pronounces *there* as *thar* and *fire* as *far* and uses many Ocracoke vocabulary items, but she has adopted the mainland use of *like* to introduce a quote, as in "I was *like*, 'I'm talking to you.'" This use of *like* is a relatively recent innovation that has spread across the mainland remarkably quickly, in just about two decades. So when Candy Gaskill employs it along with traditional island forms, she proves that her particular version of the brogue is a mixture of old and new elements. Thus, Candy Gaskill is a good example of a second-generation speaker in the three-generation dialect death process.

Besides talking about their dialect with outsiders, islanders also perform the brogue, often using set phrases that are designed to highlight many of the dialect features they're so proud of. We have heard Rex O'Neal, a likable fisherman, carpenter, and local personality who "never met a stranger," repeat the phrase "It's hoi toide on the saind soide" countless times in the few years we have known him. He is well aware of its effect on people: ordinary dingbatters, reporters, and dialect researchers all love to talk to him because he can sure "say a word." For example, one of the first things he uttered when he met Walt Wolfram was his stock performance phrase. He later told the story of this meeting to one of our fieldworkers:

Rex: I got him [Walt Wolfram] going with that "hoi toide on the saind soide."

Fieldworker: What did he say to that? Did he get all excited?

Rex: Oh my God, yeah. Came out there, said, "I'm studying speech." And I said, "Well, it's *hoi toide on the saind soide*. Last night the water *far*; tonight the moon shine. No *feesh*. What do you suppose the matter, Uncle Woods?" Well, he got a laugh out of that.

Rex O'Neal's classic saying is filled with the most marked pronunciation features of the brogue, including the *oy* sound in *hoi* and *toide*, the *ee* in *feesh*, the *ar* sound in *far* for *fire*, and the shift of the *ow* in *sound* into more of an *ay*, as in *say*.

And Rex O'Neal is not the only one who performs the brogue—maybe more often than he really speaks it. Other middle-aged and younger speakers also use the traditional dialect chiefly for performance, whether for telling humorous stories about fishermen and other island characters or for showing off the uniqueness of the language. Many members of the younger generations feel that the brogue has become almost too "quaint," too much an object of curiosity, to be used in situations in which the focus is not on language itself. The fact that the brogue is changing from the language of everyday use into a faintly remembered dialect that is rarely spoken except for display warns us that it is indeed endangered.

WHY SAVE THE BROGUE?

So what if the brogue should die? Some critics, including teachers, would breathe a sigh of relief if they never heard another Ocracoke verb or an island vowel pronunciation, especially if they thought it was simply bad English to begin with. Those who have bought into the stereotypes that associate traditional dialects with "country bumpkins" and folks "lost in time" would be happy to free islanders from these stereotypes by getting rid of the object of ridicule—their dialect. When it comes to dialects, there are still plenty of people who consider anything other than standard broadcast English uncivilized and uncouth. We know many islanders whose unfortunate encounters with language prejudices have made them wary of how outsiders view their language. And we have even encountered some who accept the stereotypes. If enough people tell you negative things about your way of life, including your language, it's hard to avoid believing them on some level. So why not let the brogue run its course and get on with life in the twenty-first century?

It would be a pity if the brogue simply washed away in the flood of outsiders inundating Ocracoke, for several reasons. To people interested in dialects, the brogue represents a chance to study certain features of the English language that can't be found anywhere else in the mainland United States, at least not nowadays. Where else in this country can you hear vowels that sound more British than American? Where else can you find a mosaic of old language traits blended so artistically with new ones? The dialect gives us a picture of the way the language once was, even as it shows us how languages change over time. When we study the brogue, we learn not only about a modern-day English dialect but also about the history of the ever changing English language.

Linguists who study language changes don't have the luxury of capturing speakers and holding them in isolated laboratories to monitor them and their descendants for several generations. That would be cruel and unusual punishment, although a researcher did once propose a study in which he would take a group of volunteers who spoke different languages to an uninhabited island to see how one common language is created from a number of different ones. Not surprisingly, he never received the funding to conduct this study, and linguists continue to rely on the real world of language as their laboratory. So when they find special situations of isolation and change, they try to take advantage of them. Islanders may take their dialect for granted, but it offers a unique window into the extraordinary world of language diversity for those of us who study languages for a living. Such situations can't be replicated once they are gone. We admit that this is a selfish consideration that serves linguists more than it benefits the people of the island, but it certainly is a good scientific justification for preserving the brogue.

There is also a cultural reason for endorsing preservation. As we have said before, language is culture, and to lose a language is to diminish a culture. This fact is generally recognized with reference to entire languages, but it is not usually acknowledged when it comes to dialects. Even islanders don't immediately call the dialect to mind when they think of the Ocracoke way of life. Just about everyone we talked to on Ocracoke said that islanders are identified first and foremost by being island born and bred. As one islander put it, "An O'cocker, a native, is somebody that's lived here; born here, their family's born here." Most people don't point to the brogue as the ultimate mark of an Ocracoker. Candy Gaskill, who seems to be a good barometer for the feelings of islanders, says it well: "It's not the brogue that's home; it's the people and the warmth, you know, the love and the community, the togetherness and stuff. I mean, I don't really think it's the brogue or the dialect, I think it's more the people that makes it."

Most islanders would agree with Candy. But they also recognize that the dialect has been a traditional symbol of their heritage. James Barrie Gaskill, Candy's father and a local merchant, fisherman, and active leader in the preservation efforts on the island, put it succinctly as he mused about the future of his young son, Morton, on the island: "I got a little kid, see, he's four weeks old; by the time he gets grown, his accent will be what they call 'dingbattish.' But I would like for him to keep the same accent and heritage that we've had for years and years; but all this is gone now. The only way we can preserve it is for you fellers to put it on tape."

The link between dialect and culture is even reflected in comments by younger members of the community. One of the youngest Ocracokers we interviewed told us that the Ocracoke dialect was "sacred, really, the way we talk; it's something the island is special for." So islanders do have some awareness of the social meaning of the dialect, even though they don't use the brogue as the basis for defining themselves as O'cockers. We can virtually guarantee that a sense of cultural loss will be felt as the brogue vanishes. The interrelatedness of dialect and culture may not be uppermost in Ocracokers' minds, but the brogue is as much a part of the island landscape as the Creek, the lighthouse, and the Atlantic Ocean. After all, language is one of the most significant and enduring emblems of human culture—and of humanity itself.

CELEBRATING THE BROGUE

Can the brogue be revived? From time to time, languages and dialects have been recovered just when they seemed on the brink of extinction. In a few cases,

James Barrie Gaskill and his son Morton inspect crab pots. (Photograph by Ann Sebrell Ehringhaus)

they have even been brought back after they died. For example, spoken Hebrew was resurrected in Israel, and Irish, which is a separate language unrelated to Irish English, is being revived in particular neighborhoods of Ireland. There are also some examples of dialects that rose, apparently from their deathbeds, to flourish again, more alive than ever. According to some linguists, African

American English is now a much more distinct dialect than it was a half-century ago.

On Martha's Vineyard, an island off the coast of Massachusetts that is well known as an upscale tourist mecca, the traditional dialect is marked by two pronunciations reminiscent of the Ocracoke brogue, in which words like *ride* are rendered as something like *ruh-eed* and *loud* as *luh-ood*. At one point several decades ago, these traditional pronunciations began fading from use in the face of increasing tourism from the mainland. But the trend reversed itself and the older, original pronunciations returned with a vengeance. Interestingly, this reversal was led by a group of middle-aged island men who had left the island for a college education. When these men returned, though, they reverted to the local pronunciation as a way of reasserting their original island identity. This resurrection of the dialect seems to have been effected in reaction to the tourism that threatened to submerge the island's distinctiveness.

We witnessed a situation similar to the Martha's Vineyard scenario among some of the middle-aged men of Ocracoke. Dave Esham, owner of the Pony Island Motel and a local poker player of some renown—at least according to his own pronouncements—left the island after high school to attend college and graduate school. After earning an M.B.A., he took a job with a prestigious accounting firm in Raleigh. But he hated land-locked life in the state capital and moved back to Ocracoke. Upon his return, he became more of an islander than ever, and his magnified brogue signaled that he was home for good.

The same story could be told of other island men. James Barrie Gaskill was one of the first islanders to graduate from college. He is also one of the most steadfast adherents of the brogue. In fact, locals often mention James Barrie when asked about good examples of brogue speakers, and he was one of the first people we went to when we arrived on the island. He too claims to be an exceptional poker player, a trait that seems to unite some of these brogue-speaking stalwarts.

But even though a small group of middle-aged men has chosen to adopt a strong version of the brogue, the Ocracoke dialect is not really regaining its former vitality, because the reversal of its decline has not been carried forward by the younger generation. It seems, rather, to be undergoing a temporary shift, a

David Esham outside the Pony Island Motel. (Photograph by Ann Sebrell Ehringhaus)

kind of last gasp before the brogue is drowned in the overwash of outside dialects. Dialects that come back from the brink of extinction are the exceptions rather than the rule. The social forces that propel attempts to revive a dying dialect or language have to be very strong indeed for a true resuscitation to take place.

One thing is for sure. If the brogue is to rise from its deathbed, its resurrection must come from a movement within the community. It will not come from dingbatter dialect revivalists like us. People who study dialects for a living have their own romantic notions—and their own biases—about preservation. Dialects, like biological species, are caught between the inevitable progression of change on the one hand and our desire to preserve them on the other. Preserving a dialect involves balancing the demands of the present with the reality of the past and prospects for the future.

It is frequently true that longtime residents of a community may see as commonplace some cultural resources that outsiders consider to be valuable treasures. What we as linguists can do, in the face of the imminent death of the Ocracoke brogue, is work with the community to promote an understanding of and appreciation for the dialect. We have tried to promote such an awareness in several ways. First, we have documented the dialect as it existed in the speech of the oldest Ocracoke residents and as it is changing among the younger generations. This is a fascinating project in itself, regardless of what happens in the future. We have interviewed and recorded more than seventy O'cockers ranging in age from ten to ninety-one. With the permission of the people interviewed, we have also put together excerpts of the spoken language for the historical record. The tape and typescript are available through the North Carolina Language and Life Project at North Carolina State University. Copies are also available at the Ocracoke School, the museum run by the Ocracoke Preservation Society, and various other museums in the Outer Banks area, including the Outer Banks Museum in Manteo.

One of our most concentrated efforts to help Ocracokers celebrate their dialect has taken place in the Ocracoke School—the smallest K-12 school in the state, even though its ranks have now swelled to nearly a hundred students. For the past several years, we have been teaching a week-long course on the dialect as a part of the social studies curriculum. This experimental unit on the Ocracoke brogue is part of the students' study of North Carolina history. Certainly the patchwork of North Carolina dialects, including those from the Outer Banks, is as important an element of North Carolina history as any other part of its heritage.

One objective of our curriculum is to raise consciousness about language and language diversity and to honestly confront the many stereotypes that surround this subject. The myths about dialects and language that have been perpetuated in our society are probably akin to a modern science teacher claiming that the planet Earth is flat. We need to raise consciousness about the dialect among students, older O'cockers, and tourists alike in order to fight some of the prejudices islanders have faced on account of their different speech. Ocracoker Joan O'Neal Johnson discussed the dilemma often faced by islanders when they move off-island. In a recent electronic mail message sent to our office, she observed:

> I recently graduated from the University of North Carolina at Wilmington with a degree in English. Currently, I am teaching at North Brunswick High School in Leland, NC. I have a great interest in the unique dialect of my people. Family members and friends have told me of your study. I have encountered both prejudice and delight at my way of speaking. During my freshman year at East Carolina University, I had a professor tell me not to write like I speak. She proceeded to tell me how ignorant I was for using a "southern" dialect. She obviously didn't know the difference in an "Ocracoke" and a "southern" dialect. Anyhow, I take pride in writing poetry about my island. When I write poems, I use the grammar and phrases that I was raised with and people like it. I believe you have helped to raise the consciousness of Ocracokers. And, I think you have given hope to my generation and to the generations to follow—letting us know that it is truly alright to be different.

To linguists who study dialects, such responses are a delight and a gratification.

Our Ocracoke students also study dialects as a type of scientific inquiry. They gather data, make hypotheses about dialect patterning, and check out their hypotheses. They learn how to figure out for themselves the dialect patterns in the materials we present to them. It's a unique discovery process, one that opens up a window into the regular and predictable nature of language in general and dialect patterning in particular. Along the way, these students also learn to think about language in new ways and to appreciate the distinctiveness of their own dialect. In other words, they develop the very "higher order thinking skills" that are ostensibly so much in demand in our educational system today.

The students are not simply passive observers of language variation but are active collectors and researchers of the Ocracoke brogue. In one exercise, they are sent out into the community to ask older relatives and neighbors about dialect words. They figure out which age groups use which words, and the information they gather allows them to see for themselves how the language is changing. In another exercise, the students investigate the patterns governing the special use of *weren't* in sentences like "I *weren't* there yesterday." As they gather their own dialect data, they begin to realize that dialects are indeed intricately patterned systems, not just "bad English." As one eighth-grader put it after a week of studying the dialect: "Studying dialect is a lot more involved than what I realized. It has a lot of grammar rules in it. I do think dialect is important here. I'm glad I get to study more on the subject with the class. I feel like our dialect is dying out and with you coming here, you will hopefully make us realize that our dialect is unique. I'm very interested in dialects."

And the students aren't the only ones who confront their own stereotypical notions about the brogue. As Gail Hamilton, the eighth-grade teacher, said about our dialect curriculum: "I appreciate it personally, not just from the children's aspect of learning about their own language, but I didn't realize there was a pattern. As an English teacher, when they would talk to me I would cringe at what I considered 'bad grammar.' Showing me that there is a specific pattern, a method of speech, is something that now I'm really proud that they know."

The students are starting to realize that their dialect is an important symbol of their island heritage. As another eighth-grader noted, "It is good to know why our dialect is so special and why we should be proud of it." The school as a whole has caught some of the dialect fever these eighth-graders feel. In fact, an entire issue of the school newspaper, the *Ocracoke Island News* (vol. 11, no. 3, 1995), was dedicated to the brogue. Student journalists turned the tables on us: they interviewed our research team and wrote a feature article about the dialect project from their perspective. The sixth-grade class wrote poems and essays about the brogue. Most of these writings included some dialect words, as in this offering from Ashley Garrish:

Ocracoke Brogue is the way
O-cockers say what they say.

If they say "I feel quamished"
It means they feel mommucked.
People make fun of how we speak.
Both of these words just mean 'weak'.
Instead of saying "It's not straight"
"It's catawampus" is how we abbreviate.
Some of our words are weird to say
And some can be hard to state.
Such as a wampus cat is the island rogue,
Well that is my poem on the Ocracoke Brogue.   (p. 18)

In addition to our work in the school, we have also produced a twenty-five-minute documentary video titled *The Ocracoke Brogue*. This film aims to be both entertaining and informative and is designed for public, popular viewing—by residents and tourists both—as well as for educational purposes. We have shown our documentary in the school and at a meeting of the Ocracoke Preservation Society. We also showed it several times at Howard's Pub, the popular bar and grill where community members and tourists often congregate. It also was part of an exhibit on the Ocracoke brogue in the Ocracoke Historical Preservation Society Museum that was viewed by countless tourists visiting the island. These showings sparked animated, positive discussions about the dialect by both islanders and tourists.

The students have been joined by teachers and community members in collecting and documenting the dialect. For example, Candy Gaskill and Chester Lynn patiently tolerated all manner of dingbatter questions as we sat around the table at Albert Styron's General Store, collecting examples and taking notes on dialect words—the words now included in the dialect dictionary in Chapter 2. The day after we discussed vocabulary in her class, eighth-grade teacher Gail Hamilton returned with over two pages of lexical items and phrases elicited from her elderly relatives. On another occasion, she wrote the following poem, which uses many unique Outer Banks expressions, in celebration of the dialect. These dialect expressions are italicized in the poem.

The Ocracoke Brogue

Ocracoke Tradition, Heritage and Such—
For some *dingbatters* is really too much
What is a first cousin once-removed?
Does a trip *down below* have to be approved?

Mommuck, doset, and *miserable'n the wind*
Is this *O'cock brogue* meant to offend?
When I see *wampus cat,* what do I see?
Hoi toid on the seund soid is Greek to me!

Hey, *puck* isn't used in the game of hockey.
Do *O'cockers* "hoid" when playing *meehonkey*?
While on your *pizer,* do you sit for *a spell*?
If you go *down below,* do you go to . . . well?

Been a *whit* since I took a *scud across the beach.*
Things get *catawampus* if they're hard to reach.
Every *whipstitch* the *Creek* gets *slick cam*
If you're not confused, well *pucker dog,* I am!

If I'm *Down Point* or *Up Trent,* where'll I be?
Well, *Bucky,* it's still *good-some* to me!
Some may get *quamish* from the attention,
But this Brogue's too unique not to mention.   (March 1995)

Gail Hamilton's clever incorporation of so many dialect words into her poem is inspiring to those who are concerned about the fate of the Ocracoke brogue, but maybe even more important than this teacher's newfound appreciation is the change in student attitudes toward the traditional Ocracoke dialect. When Hamilton was asked about the effect of the dialect curriculum on her students, she remarked: "The pride that has been established is phenomenal— the rate of the self-esteem increasing, pride in the uniqueness of the way they speak. It has been such a positive experience for them. Before, when foreigners, tourists, would come down, it was something they were ashamed of, because

Teacher Gail Hamilton and students participating in the Dialect Awareness Curriculum. (Photograph by Ann Sebrell Ehringhaus)

they talked differently. And so now, with pride, they say, 'Hoi toide on the sound soide.'"

Despite these encouraging signs of a new awareness of and a heightened respect for the brogue, though, its fate is still undecided. Circumstances beyond the community's direct control will probably determine its ultimate fortune. But the islanders are definitely beginning to realize their rich dialect tradition and the linguistic and cultural stakes involved in the death of the brogue. We as linguists may not be able to do more to save the brogue than can its speakers, but if nothing else, we have chronicled for the historical record, for curious outsiders, and for concerned community members the nature of this once-vibrant dialect. If the brogue dies, it will be an irrecoverable loss. But, as one of world's leading authorities on language death, Nancy Dorian, has noted, if a language or dialect dies, then the least we can do is give it a celebrated funeral. It may be ebb tide for the *hoi toide* dialect, but its legacy deserves to be indelibly preserved—for O'cockers, new Ocracoke residents, and tourists who wish to understand why the island is such a special place.

The Voices of Ocracoke

7

In this final chapter, we want to let a few O'cockers speak for themselves. Ultimately, the true flavor of Ocracoke speech can be savored only by listening to the real people who use it, not by merely describing how they speak. Therefore, it seems only appropriate that we conclude our book with a few stories and impressions from islanders. These excerpts have been selected from more than a hundred hours of tape-recorded interviews.

Reading the transcription of a story or narrative is hardly the same as hearing it firsthand—especially on Ocracoke, where the true effect of the brogue depends heavily on speech rhythms and the nuances of certain vowel sounds. We can't capture such subtleties in writing, especially as we have opted to follow standard spellings in the narratives below. Readers can only imagine how each story might sound based on our foregoing description of the dialect—or, if they're lucky, they might hear the Ocracoke dialect firsthand.

We have chosen to present the narratives of only four Ocracokers. More can be heard on the North Carolina Language and Life Project's archival tape. The four speakers presented here, two men and two women, are well-known O'-cockers who were extremely helpful to us during the course of our study. The excerpts that follow give us insight not only into how speakers put together their stories and descriptions but also into how they remember the past—when the brogue was alive and well and Ocracoke was for O'cockers.

HURRICANES, HOGS, AND HANGOVERS
by Essie O'Neal

Essie O'Neal, age seventy-nine at the time of our interview with her, is one of Ocracoke's premier storytellers. As they say on the island, "She can say a word, now." Essie O'Neal is the mother of eleven O'Neal sons, so she understandably has plenty of stories to tell. The following narratives are just two of the many she told us during our two-hour interview. They focus on two themes common in Ocracoke narratives—the weather and animals. The first story is about the hurricane of 1944, one of the most severe storms ever weathered by the island. Most people who lived through it can still remember it vividly. But only a few people recall the story of the hog who survived the storm in a trunk. Or the second story of the hog who went on a drunk.

I had a new maple bedroom set. I had just got it in the house three or four days, when this storm come—the '44 storm. It come all the sudden. We had a pretty day, just like this. No wind, pretty sunshine. And the neighbor called that day and said, "There's a bad storm a-heading right straight for us." We didn't believe it. "There ain't no storm, there ain't no storm come."
She said, "Yes, it's headed right straight for Cape Hatteras."
It was a pretty, calm day; and that night, after it got to dark good, I went out with Harry, went out on the porch, and the stars was shining. He says, "I don't think there's no storm. It don't look like a storm." Everything was calm. But let me tell you, when we woke up the next morning, I thought the roof was gonna

Essie O'Neal in her front yard. (Photograph by Ann Sebrell Ehringhaus)

come off the house. I never heard such a hard wind — blowing a hundred miles. I never heard such a hard wind.

Harry said, "You better get up and get all them kids ready and get them dressed. We'll have to leave here."

I was working as fast as I could to get them all and put them to the table, give them breakfast and everything. Harry looked and the tide was a-rolling right in the yard. It come up so fast; it was a-rolling in the yard. And that's when we left. When we left out of that gate, I tell you, it was about four foot of water in the gate when we left out. We had to leave there in a boat.

But anyway, we had a half-grown pig, and Harry didn't want him to drown, and he put him in a ole big wooden trunk, one of them big ole-timey trunks. So he put him in that trunk and put the trunk on the porch. I said, "That pig will float around in that trunk; he'll think he's in a boat."

So, when the tide all run off that evening late, Harry said "I'm going up to the house, to see if we got a house." We didn't even think we had a house.

I said, "Can we go?"

"No," he said, "You better stay here, wait till I go."

So, when he come back, he said, "I saw the house was standing, but the door was wide open—had blowed open. And the first thing I met was the pig coming out of the living room." He said, "That pig come out of that living room, I thought he was going to knock me down, he run so fast, he's so scared."

I went in the bedroom, and, honey, he had with his hoofs cut that maple bedstead all to pieces. I had to throw it out; it wasn't no good anymore. He'd ruined that bedstead. I told him, I said, "Don't ever get another pig! 'Cause these young'uns is enough for to take care of, without taking care of a pig."

We had another pig, a little red pig, and he broke the pen and got out of that pen. But the men had made meal wine [wine made from cornmeal and fruit]; they had made this meal wine in a tank or big five-gallon jars. When they all drinked it, they scraped it off. They just had settlings, the meal and the peaches, or whatever they put in it.

Harry took the settlings and everything and dumped them in the hog trough. And the hog eat 'em, and he got drunk! You ever seen a drunk hog? This hog, he run all around up and down all over the house and jumped on the porch and jumped in. We couldn't catch him. Everybody run him around and couldn't catch that hog. And he was a-running and running, just all around, just crazy, turning somersaults. My sister had started there, was gonna help me wash. Just as she got to the gate, the hog was coming out. I called, I said, "Stop!" I said. "Just stop! Wait!" She didn't know what I meant, and all that time that hog run, and he run right through her legs and turned her over backwards, and kept on going down the road, and she screamed. It scared her.

We didn't see that hog in two days. He never come back or nothing. But it was two days, and it were two Coast Guard boys come to the door and knocked on the door. I went and one of them said, "Harry lives here, don't he?"

I said, "Harry O'Neal?"

He said, "I would like to have him to come down to the Coast Guard station."

I thought something really bad was wrong. I said, "Well, I'll tell him, I'll tell him when he comes back."

He said, "We want to see if he can identify a hog."

When Harry come from work, I told him, I said, "They want you down the Coast Guard station."

"For what?" he said.

I said, "They got a hog down there, they want you to identify it."

He said "What? I better go now then." So he left, and it was that hog of his. They had spotted him from the cupola—swimming. He was swimming towards Portsmouth. They saw this red thing and thought it was somebody a-red-headed. They thought it was a person. They went after it with a P.T. boat. They went after it, said, "There's a person overboard over there!" They could see its head. It could have been a red-headed person. And when they went after it, it was that hog. They thought it was a person. It was over there by the Hog Shoal, they got a shoal over there named Hog Shoal. That's where the hog was at, where they got him over to Hog Shoal.

They brought him home and they put him in the pen. Well, we get out there and poured his food in his trough, that they supposed to have, like middlings and stuff. He wouldn't eat it. He just laid down and slept. All that day he didn't eat nothing, and just laid and slept. We had to go dump that old food out and put new in, and he still wouldn't eat. He still laid there. So, Harry come home again that evening for supper, he said, "Did he eat anything? Did the hog eat anything?"

I said, "No, he hain't," I said. "He hain't moved," and I said, "He's still a-laying there."

He said, "Well, if you had a hangover like he's got, you would lay there too."

AN AIRPORT OYSTER SPILL
by Rex O'Neal

Rex O'Neal, thirty-nine at the time of our interview with him, is the second-youngest son of Essie O'Neal. He is a carpenter, fisherman, and island personality. He is also a great conversationalist with an engaging sense of humor and a flair for entertaining. The following story recounts an incident that took place on one of the off-island excursions Rex and his friends make every year. To get the true flavor of the story, you need to envision an animated storyteller who punctuates his tales with lots of sweeping gestures and exaggerated facial expressions—and who enjoys his own stories as much as his listeners do. Our transcription is based on a couple of separate tellings of Rex's now-famous "Oyster Story," which is fast becoming a part of island lore.

We get a group every year, for twelve years. Usually we just ride up to Atlantic City, and right after the New Year's is over, we just take a long weekend. Usually all the guys get together, about seven or eight of us. We'll usually take up a bushel of oysters or something with us. We get a couple of styrofoam coolers and put 'em in there and put ice into the bottom and put newspapers on top of them and wrap them up with duct tape. And take them right up to the room and set right in the room and eat raw oysters in the room and stuff like that.

Well, we went to Vegas about three years ago.

Somebody said, "What are we gonna do about oysters?"

I said, "Hell with it, we're still gonna take them anyways." So we get these styrofoam coolers, put ice in the bottom, put oysters on. When we get to the airport, we say, "Well, here's some more luggage!" And we shipped them on the plane right along with the rest of our luggage. So three o'clock in the morning, we get to the airport. We go out to the chute where your luggage is shooting out, and the chute was throwing these suitcases from about three feet down. It was one of those ones that shoots it off right here. I went, "Shit! I better get there and get a-hold of that dang cooler when it comes. If I don't I'm gonna lose our oysters!"

Sure enough, here come the cooler around. So about time it comes, getting

Rex O'Neal and David Esham "saying a word" at the poker house.
(Photograph by Ann Sebrell Ehringhaus)

ready to come off of that chute, I grab it so it won't throw it off there. And about time I grab it, it folds, the bottom falls out of it. And these oysters, they all take off going running all back around the belt, all back around the belt. Which interrupts everybody's luggage. About forty or fifty people standing there waiting for their luggage. And everybody that's with me—there's like a group of ten of us—they all scampered. They all haul ass. Everybody leaves me right there holding that broken cooler. So here the oysters go. They come back by. I seen 'em coming back, and I say, "I wonder what I'm gonna put 'em in."

Some lady comes up and hands me this here box. She finds me this tote thing to put them in, so I grab them when they come by, start putting about four or five in, and they're gone again. I got to wait till the next time around. Next time they come around, she jumps in there and is helping me. Everyone else done left in the meantime. This one woman looks at it, she says, "What are they, clams?"

I said, "No, they're oysters." About the third or fourth time around, I got about seven or eight people there helping me, not a-one of them that was with me helping. We finally get them up. I thought they was gonna run us out of the airport.

I waited there for the next batch, mixed in with everybody's luggage. And the other batch never did show up. They musta busted somewhere else before they got that far.

I gave my friends a cussing for hauling ass on me. I want to tell you that.

THE WAY THINGS WERE
by Elizabeth Howard

Elizabeth Howard, who was eighty-two when we interviewed her, was one of the most respected of all O'cockers. When she died at age eighty-four during the winter of 1996, the island community lost one of its most beloved treasures, as well as a fine role model for younger islanders. As one Ocracoker put it, "Everybody loves Elizabeth." Warm, congenial, and generous, she could engage listeners in conversation for hours as she sat on the porch, or *pizer*, of her house near the British Cemetery. She was the first person we interviewed on Ocracoke in the early 1990s, and she set the tone for our reception into the community. Her family was one of the first to settle on the island, and they have been an integral part of its culture for generations. Her father ran the general store, and as a young girl Elizabeth would help him. She later ran the post office. In the following account, taken from that first interview we conducted on Ocracoke, she tells about outsiders' perceptions of the island and the way things really were back in the old days.

I have known some girls and boys too, that went away to school. And they would not tell anybody they were from Ocracoke. I guess we were isolated, and maybe somebody had laughed at something they'd said. I've always told them that I was from Ocracoke. People did not know where Ocracoke was. When I

Elizabeth Howard by her picket fence. (Photograph by Ann Sebrell Ehringhaus)

went to school in Angier, my daddy sent a barrel full of oysters in the shell to me, and I gave them all around in that neighborhood. Well, of course they didn't know how to open oysters. Nobody there had the oyster knife. They had to use any kind of knife they had. And they'd hit them with a hammer to break the shell. They had never been to an island as far as that's concerned. In fact, even up in Maryland, one time this lady, she asked me where I was from, and I told her Ocracoke Island, and she said, "You live on an island?"

I said, "Yes, I do."

She sort of frowned, like she thought that was terrible. "Well, what do you eat?"

I said, "Well, honey, you name it, and we eat it."

Now I've been everywhere, I think, but I have never been anywhere people eat any better than they do here on the island. They had everything to eat, too. They have the seafood and they have the vegetation. People had cows. They had sheep. My daddy had a lot of sheep. He had a lot of cattle down on the banks. They stayed there, they're wild. He had both cattle and sheep, and he had horses too. I love horses.

I was raised in a yard with three horses, and there's several girls that lived in the neighborhood. We used to put two wood boxes, one on top of the other, and climb up one of our horses, one that was very, very tame. Bill had been a old racehorse. When we would go anywhere, and old Bill would be hitched to the cart, that horse would poke, poke wherever we went. Just go slow. But when we'd start to home, that horse would trot. How did that horse know we're coming home? It's that instinct in it.

A WILD ISLAND AND WILD PONIES
by James Barrie Gaskill

James Barrie Gaskill, forty-nine when we interviewed him, has served the island in many different capacities—store owner, fisherman, school principal, school janitor, preservation society officer, environmental activist, and poker player, among others. However, nothing seems to please him more than tending his crab pots during the first days of spring. Although he was one of the first college graduates on the island, he still speaks the brogue, and speaks it proudly. He is saddened by the loss of cultural heritage brought on by the fading of the brogue. He is a ready source of information and island perspective and is amazingly tolerant of all manner of inquiry from those who frequent the business he co-owns, Albert Styron's General Store. In the following passage, he talks about

James Barrie Gaskill wonders about the future of the brogue for his son Morton's generation. (Photograph by Ann Sebrell Ehringhaus)

life on the island when hunting was an everyday occurrence and even the ponies and cattle ran wild — except when they were penned.

There weren't all this swamp here. We had beaches before everybody started building; you'd have beach all the way around on the sound side, just like you do on the ocean. But now you don't. Everybody's breakwatered and filled in. All these houses from where we turned at the fire station up this way has been built here since the 1960s.

We were shooting shotguns when we were ten, eleven year old. There wadn't nothing around here but all island. I'd just leave home and walk right on through the woods and go duck hunting and get back in time for school. When you get out evenings, you'd run home or come home on your bicycle just as quick as you could, then go hunting till dark. There weren't no law out here, didn't pay any attention to the season or anything. You'd eat everything you killed. You really didn't kill no more than what you wanted. You might go out and kill five or six ducks or three or four geese a day. But you'd give 'em away to the older people in the neighborhood. But the best eating of all was these beach birds—these birds you see down on the ocean, especially the ones they call red knots, or red breasts.

We used to have a pony penning every Fourth of July. See, the horses run wild. You'd go down the night before, the ones that was gonna drive the horses or the ponies back. They'd go on the north end and camp out and then start daylight next morning. There was five or six different bunches. Each stallion had anywhere from eight, ten, fifteen mares. They stayed in groups, and you'd start penning 'em. The one group would catch up to the other. They'd fight all the way up, come in all the way up to the penning. The last pony penning they had was right out where the new part of the Island Inn is now.

We just rode a horse. We started on that end and started running 'em back this way. Then the ponies would come around, you'd pen 'em up, and they'd come right on the shore out there. We had about two hundred fifty to three hundred head of cattle running wild on the island. People brought 'em here and left them. They didn't brand them. But the horses, they branded them. Everybody had a mark. They'd cut so many notches out of the ear. My father, he had one ear on the cow. It was half cut off on this side. And on the other side, he had a hole through it and then a couple of nips. Different ones had different marks.

Appendix

An Ocracoke IQ Test
Or, How to Tell a Dingbatter from an O'cocker

Now that you have been through the book, you might want to test your newfound expertise in the brogue by taking the following vocabulary quiz. We have referred to some of these words regularly throughout the book; others we introduced only in our discussion of Ocracoke vocabulary in Chapter 2. We devised this exercise simply for fun, to illustrate the diversity of Ocracoke vocabulary. At the same time, however, it also demonstrates how vocabulary can be very culturally specific. Interestingly, this test is not unlike the kinds of tests routinely used to assess students' language aptitude and proficiency in school—except that most of those tests are restricted to mainstream, mainland English. If nothing else, the quiz should help us appreciate how our vocabulary is molded by our environment, and how relative it can be.

To take the quiz, choose the word or phrase that most closely defines each term. The answers are given at the end of the quiz. Give yourself one point for each correct response. Then rate your proficiency in the brogue according to the Ocracoke IQ scale that follows the answer key.

1. **dingbatter**
   a. a baseball player in a small boat
   b. a husband
   c. a wife
   d. an outsider

2. **up the beach**
   a. by the sea
   b. north of the island
   c. the national parkland area
   d. Oyster Creek

3. **meehonkey**
   a. a call used in hide-and-seek
   b. a call made to attract ducks
   c. the call of an angry person
   d. an island marsh plant

4. **quamish**
   a. an upset stomach
   b. a fearful feeling
   c. a bad headache
   d. an excited feeling

5. **pizer**
   a. a small boat
   b. a deck
   c. a porch
   d. a small Italian pie with cheese

6. **mommuck** (also spelled **mammock**)
      a. to imitate someone
      b. to bother someone
      c. to make fun of someone
      d. to become close friends with someone

7. She's **to** the restaurant.
      a. She ate at the restaurant twice.
      b. She's been to the restaurant.
      c. She's at the restaurant.
      d. She's going to the restaurant.

8. **fladget**
      a. gas in the alimentary canal
      b. an island men's game
      c. a small island bird
      d. a small piece of something

9. **puck**
      a. a small disk used in island hockey games
      b. a sweetheart
      c. a kiss on the cheek
      d. a mischievous person

10. **O'cocker**
      a. a derogatory term for an Ocracoker
      b. a outsider's mispronunciation of the term **Ocracoker**
      c. an island term for a native Ocracoker
      d. an island term for bluefish

11. **token of death**
      a. a coin needed for admission to Hades
      b. a sickness leading to death

c. a fatal epidemic

d. an unusual event that forecasts a death

12. louard

a. lowering an anchor

b. an exaggerated exclamation, as in "louard have mercy"

c. moving away from the wind

d. a fatty substance

13. Russian rat

a. a unique island rodent

b. an island gossip

c. a vodka-drinking narc

d. a mink

14. Hatterasser

a. a storm that blows in from Hatteras

b. a ferry ride from Ocracoke to Hatteras

c. a person from Hatteras

d. a fishing trip in Hatteras Inlet

15. the Ditch

a. a small body of water behind the general store

b. the mouth of Silver Lake harbor

c. another name for the Pamlico Sound

d. the island's largest skeeter breeding ground

16. scud

a. a dirty person

b. a tire mark in the sand

c. a ride in a car or boat

d. a missile

17. **doast**
     a. sick, especially with the flu
     b. a square dance step
     c. a small crab
     d. toast, especially wheat bread

18. **fatback**
     a. bacon
     b. an overweight Hatterasser
     c. an island pig
     d. menhaden, a type of oily fish

19. **goaty**
     a. a small beard on the chin
     b. smelling foul, like a goat
     c. having the appearance of a goat
     d. silly

20. **slick cam**
     a. a well-oiled engine part
     b. greased down hair
     c. a glossy picture
     d. very still water

ANSWERS:

1. d	6. b	11. d	16. c
2. b	7. c	12. c	17. a
3. a	8. d	13. a	18. d
4. a	9. b	14. c	19. b
5. c	10. c	15. b	20. d

RATE YOUR OCRACOKE IQ:

0–5 = a complete dingbatter
6–10 = an educable dingbatter
11–15 = an average O'cocker
16–20 = an island genius

References and Bibliographic Notes

Several kinds of sources have provided the information for our description of the Ocracoke brogue. As with most descriptive dialect studies, we relied most heavily on tape-recorded interviews. Over a three-year period, we recorded interviews with more than seventy Ocracokers, ranging in age from ten to ninety-one years old. Our interviews, typically lasting from one to two hours each, generally involved discussions about topics that varied from childhood games to current activities on the island. Our goal was simply to engage people in casual conversation so that we could obtain a sample of relatively informal speech. Although we are interested in a range of speech styles, casual conversation usually proves to be the most useful for a description of the primary dialect. Our open-ended style of interviewing also enabled us to gather background information that helped us set the context for our language study. Following the conversational portion of the interview, we usually asked some direct questions about specific dialect features—particular words, sentence structures, and pronunciations.

Many of these interviews were fully transcribed by staff members of the North Carolina Language and Life Project at North Carolina State University. Following the word-by-word transcriptions, we spent countless hours listening to the small details of pronunciation and grammar. In some cases, we noted every instance of a particular pronunciation or sentence structure in the interview. For example, we noted the exact pronunciation of every instance of the *i* vowel in words like *tide* or *time* in the speech of nearly twenty-five speakers. We then summarized how frequently each pronunciation was used. In studying pronunciation, we double-checked our listening skills with instruments that measure the sound waves of speech, such as the Computer Speech Lab produced by Kay Elemetrics. Such techniques helped us greatly as we sought to describe precisely the vowels of Outer Banks English.

We complemented our study of Ocracoke speech with a comparative study of Harkers Island, where we have interviewed nearly fifty different people over the past couple of years. The examination of another Outer Banks dialect helps us determine the dialect similarities and differences among Ocracoke and other Outer Banks communities.

We were able to extend our comparison to island communities beyond the Outer Banks by including a set of interviews with more than forty speakers from Smith Island, Maryland, thereby giving us an idea of how the dialect structures of Ocracoke relate to dialects in other historically isolated island communities along the eastern seaboard—in this case, the Chesapeake Bay area. Rebecca Setliff, who conducted the interviews on Smith Island in the early 1980s, generously loaned us her tapes for our comparative study.

In order to compare the Ocracoke brogue with mainland dialects, we have been conducting interviews with residents in a number of mainland North Carolina communities. For example, in the last two years, we have interviewed more than eighty people in Robeson County representing the Native American, European American, and African American dialect communities. We have also interviewed more than forty speakers representing both the African American and European American communities in Warren County. More recently, we have begun interviewing Native Americans whose first language is Cherokee in Graham County in the western part of the state. We continue to add to our repository of interviews throughout the state on a regular basis. By doing so, we are striving to paint dialect pictures of particular, representative types of North Carolina communities in an effort to arrive at an overall portrayal of the varied dialect landscape of the state. Our current studies have resulted in the publication, in professional linguistic journals, of a number of technical descriptions of specific structures in Ocracoke English and other North Carolina dialects by members of the North Carolina Language and Life Project staff. Some of these are listed in the references below.

We have supplemented our firsthand study of Ocracoke speech with available written dialect descriptions of Ocracoke and other Outer Banks islands. Despite the region's longstanding fascination for outsiders, we found only a couple of such descriptions when we embarked on this project. These include Robert Howren's "The Speech of Ocracoke, North Carolina," Hilda Jaffe's "The Speech of the Central Coast of North Carolina: The Carteret County Version of the Banks 'Brogue,'" and especially Wynne Dough's unpublished honor's thesis at the University of North Carolina–Chapel Hill, "A Preliminary Survey of the Speech of the Northern Outer Banks of North Carolina."

More general dialect surveys of the southeastern United States sometimes include a few representations of Outer Banks speech; however, these studies are more helpful in comparing the speech of various lowland and highland areas of the North Carolina mainland than they are for their characterization of Outer Banks dialects. For example, the records used in compiling the *Dictionary of American Regional English* included interviews, conducted in the 1960s, with almost a hundred residents scattered throughout North Carolina, including twelve from the Outer Banks and three from Ocracoke.

Interviews conducted before World War II in connection with the Linguistic Atlas of the Middle and South Atlantic States survey include seventy-five speakers scattered throughout North Carolina, several of whom were from the Outer Banks but none from Ocracoke. Works that evolved from the Linguistic Atlas survey include *The Pronunciation of English in the Atlantic States* (Kurath and McDavid, 1961), *Linguistic Atlas of the Middle and South Atlantic States* (McDavid and O'Cain), and the *Handbook of the Linguistic Atlas of the Middle and South Atlantic States* (Kretzschmar, McDavid, Lerud, and Johnson). An *Annotated Bibliography of Southern American English*, by James McMillan and Michael Montgomery, provides the most comprehensive listing of references for the various strands of southern speech.

Our comparison of Ocracoke English with southern highland speech is based on some of the sources mentioned above, but it relies most heavily on the original studies of Appalachian and Ozark English that Walt Wolfram and his colleagues have carried out over the past two decades. These are summarized in books such as Wolfram and Christian, *Appalachian Speech*, and Christian, Wolfram, and Dube, *Variation and Change in Geographically Isolated Communities: Appalachian and Ozark English*. Recent investigations of the continental roots of Appalachian English by Michael Montgomery have helped clarify some of the issues concerning the sources of the unique aspects of Appalachian English and, by extension, Outer Banks English.

For our comparison of Ocracoke English with dialects in the British Isles, we relied on works such as Upton, Parry, and Widdowson, *Survey of English Dialects: The Dictionary and Grammar*; Orton et al., *The Linguistic Atlas of England*; Trudgill's *Language in the British Isles*; and *The Dialects of England*. Happily, the British dialectologist Peter Trudgill was able to visit Ocracoke with us and made a number of helpful observations about the British connections with the Outer Banks.

The social and historical background for our linguistic study comes from a number of sources. Our knowledge of the region's history has been derived from works such as Stick, *The Outer Banks of North Carolina*; Shelby et al., *Hyde County History: A Hyde County Bicentennial Project*; Ballance, *Ocracokers*; and Dough, "A Preliminary Survey of the Speech of the Northern Outer Banks of North Carolina." Wynne Dough was particularly helpful because he meticulously investigated many historical sources, such as land deeds and settlement records. Alton Ballance's account offers a first-person account of Ocracoke past and present, and such a perspective is especially useful for establishing the ethnographic background of the dialect on Ocracoke. The prolific compilation of historical records by Ellen Fulcher Cloud also proved quite useful in setting the sociohistorical context of Ocracoke. For example, compilations such as *From Whence*

We Came: The History of the Original Ocracoke Names, Custom Records: Port of Ocracoke, 1815–1866, and *The Federal Census of Ocracoke Island, 1790–1910* provide records of early island families that make up our primary sample for language study.

We have complemented such social and historical sources with our own personal observations during the three-year period of our study. During regular visits and extended stays on Ocracoke over the past three years, our involvement ranged from participating in a number of different types of social activities to teaching an instructional unit on dialects in the school. Islanders generously included us in many of their activities, thus allowing us to observe the brogue in action—in the pub, in homes, on docks, in boats, and in school. We have thus attempted to combine our own observations about the sociolinguistic life of the community with documented accounts by historians and other observers of Outer Banks life.

Finally, we have been instructed by a growing interest in language endangerment within linguistics. The threatened status of a majority of the world's languages has raised language scholars' consciousness about preserving language as never before, and a rapidly expanding body of literature is being devoted to the plight of endangered languages—for scientific, cultural, and aesthetic reasons. Such linguists as Nancy Dorian, Robert Robins and Eugenius Uhlenbeck, and Ken Hale and his colleagues have documented the process of language death and the threat to the world's languages. None of their studies, however, have considered the fate of dying dialects of "healthy" languages such as the moribund Ocracoke brogue, which is being taken over by other dialects of English. Our extension of language endangerment to include endangered dialects is novel, although it seems quite natural and reasonable to us. The dialect awareness programs and preservation activities we describe in Chapter 6 are unique within the United States, although language awareness programs have now become fairly popular in some parts of Europe. The rationale for these programs is given in Wolfram, *Dialects and American English,* as well as other articles by Wolfram and Schilling-Estes. The general nature of language awareness programs is described in books such as Van Lier, *Introducing Language Awareness,* and Carter, *Knowledge about Language and the Curriculum: The LINC Reader;* these programs are also discussed on a regular basis in the journal *Language Awareness,* published by Multilingual Matters in Clevedon, England.

In compiling our picture of the Ocracoke brogue, we have tried to blend our first-hand observation of dialect patterning with research literature on language, dialect, history, and culture. Certainly there is much more to be said; we just hope that we have opened up a continuing conversation about Ocracoke's significant dialect heritage.

Ballance, Alton. *Ocracokers*. Chapel Hill: University of North Carolina Press, 1989.

Blanton, Phyllis, and Karen Waters, producers. *The Ocracoke Brogue: A Video Documentary*. Raleigh: North Carolina Language and Life Project, 1994.

Carter, Ronald, ed. *Knowledge about Language and the Curriculum: The LINC Reader*. London: Hodder and Stoughton, 1990.

Cloud, Ellen Fulcher. *Ocracoke Lighthouse*. Spartanburg, S.C.: The Reprint Company, 1993.

————. *Old Salt*. Ocracoke, N.C.: Live Oak Publications, 1995.

Creech, Kevyn, and John Creech, producers. *That Island Talk: Harkers Island Dialect*. Raleigh: American Media Productions and the North Carolina Language and Life Project, 1996.

Ehringhaus, Ann Sebrell. *Ocracoke Portrait*. Winston-Salem, N.C.: John F. Blair, 1988.

Roberts Stephens, Kay Holt. *Judgment Land: The Story of Salter Path, Book 1*. Havelock, N.C.: Bogue Sound, 1984.

Shelby, Marjorie T., et al. *Hyde County History: A Hyde County Centennial Project*. Charlotte, N.C.: Herb Eaton, Inc., 1976.

Stick, David. *Graveyard of the Atlantic: Shipwrecks of the North Carolina Coast*. Chapel Hill: University of North Carolina Press, 1952.

————. *The Outer Banks of North Carolina*. Chapel Hill: University of North Carolina Press, 1958.

Van Lier, Leo. *Introducing Language Awareness*. London: Penguin Books, 1995.

Warner, William W. *Beautiful Swimmers: Watermen, Crabs, and the Chesapeake Bay*. New York: Penguin Books, 1982.

Wilson, Charles Reagan, and William Ferris, eds. *Encyclopedia of Southern Culture*. Chapel Hill: University of North Carolina Press, 1989. See especially the following sections: "Language," edited by Michael Montgomery, pp. 757–92; and "History and Manners," edited by Charles Reagan Wilson, pp. 579–709.

Wolfram, Walt. *Dialects and American English*. Englewood Cliffs, N.J.: Prentice Hall, 1991.

Wolfram, Walt, and Natalie Schilling-Estes. *American English: Dialects and Variation*. Cambridge, Mass.: Basil Blackwell, 1997.

Cassidy, Frederic G., ed. *Dictionary of American Regional English*. 3 vols. to date. Cambridge, Mass.: Belknap Press, 1985–96.

Cheek, Davina Adrianne. "Harkers Island /ɔ/ and the Southern Norm: A Microcosm of Languages in Contact." Master's thesis, North Carolina State University, 1995.

Christian, Donna, Walt Wolfram, and Nanjo Dube. *Variation and Change in Geographically Isolated Communities: Appalachian English and Ozark English*. Publications of the American Dialect Society, no. 74. Tuscaloosa: University of Alabama Press, 1988.

Cloud, Ellen Fulcher. *Custom Records: Port of Ocracoke, 1815–1866*. Ocracoke, N.C.: Live Oak Publications, 1995.

———. *The Federal Census of Ocracoke Island, 1790–1910*. Ocracoke, N.C.: Live Oak Publications, 1995.

———. *From Whence We Came: The History of the Original Ocracoke Names*. Ocracoke, N.C.: Live Oak Publications, 1995.

Dorian, Nancy C. *Language Death: The Life Cycle of a Scottish Gaelic Dialect*. Philadelphia: University of Pennsylvania Press, 1981.

———, ed. *Investigating Obsolescence: Studies in Language Contraction and Obsolescence*. Cambridge: Cambridge University Press, 1989.

Dough, Wynne C. "A Preliminary Survey of the Speech of the Northern Outer Banks of North Carolina." Honors essay, University of North Carolina at Chapel Hill, 1982.

Hale, Ken, Michael Krauss, Lucille Watahomigie, Akira Yamamoto, Colette Craig, LaVerne Masayesva Jeanne, and Nora England. "Endangered Languages." *Language* 68 (1992): 1–42.

Hazen, Kirk. "Subject-Verb Concord in Post-Insular Vernacular Varieties of English." Master's thesis, North Carolina State University, 1994.

Howren, Robert. "The Speech of Ocracoke, North Carolina." *American Speech* 37.3 (1962): 163–75.

Hughes, Arthur, and Peter Trudgill. *English Accents and Dialects*. London: Edward Arnold, 1980.

Jaffe, Hilda. *The Speech of the Central Coast of North Carolina: The Carteret County Version of the Banks "Brogue."* Publications of the American Dialect Society, no. 60. Tuscaloosa: University of Alabama Press, 1973.

Kretzschmar, William A., Virginia G. McDavid, Thomas K. Lerud, and Ellen Johnson, eds. *Handbook of the Linguistic Atlas of the Middle and South Atlantic States.* Chicago: University of Chicago Press, 1995.

Kurath, Hans, and Raven I. McDavid. *The Pronunciation of English in the Atlantic States.* Ann Arbor, Mich., 1961.

Labov, William. *Principles of Linguistic Change: Internal Factors.* Cambridge, Mass.: Basil Blackwell, 1994.

————. "The Social Motivation of a Sound Change." *Word* 19 (1963): 273–307.

Labov, William, Malcah Yaeger, and Richard Steiner. *A Quantitative Study of Sound Change.* National Science Foundation GS-3287, 1972.

McDavid, Raven I., and Ray O'Cain. *Linguistic Atlas of the Middle and South Atlantic States.* Chicago: University of Chicago Press, 1980.

McMillan, James, and Michael Montgomery. *Annotated Bibliography of Southern American English.* Tuscaloosa: University of Alabama Press, 1989.

Montgomery, Michael. "Exploring the Roots of Appalachian English." *English World-Wide* 10 (1989): 227–78.

————. 1991. "The Roots of Appalachian English: Scotch-Irish or Southern British?" In *Journal of the Appalachian Studies Association*, edited by John Inscoe, 177–91. Johnson City: East Tennessee State University Center for Appalachian Studies and Services, 1991.

Myhill, John. "Postvocalic /r/ as an Index of Integration into the Black English Vernacular Speech Community." *American Speech* 63.3 (1988): 203–13.

Orton, Harold, Stewart Sanderson, and John Widdowson. *The Linguistic Atlas of England.* London: Croom Helm, 1978.

Pyles, Thomas, and John Algeo. *The Origins and Development of the English Language.* Orlando, Fla.: Harcourt Brace Jovanovich, 1993.

Robins, Robert H., and Eugenius M. Uhlenbeck, eds. *Endangered Languages.* Oxford: Berg, 1991.

Schilling-Estes, Natalie. "Production, Perception, and Patterning: 'Performance' Speech in an Endangered Dialect Variety." *Penn Review of Linguistics* 19 (1995): 117–31.

Schilling-Estes, Natalie, and Walt Wolfram. "Convergent Explanation and Alternative Regularization Patterns: *Were/Weren't* Leveling in a Vernacular English Variety." *Language Variation and Change* 6 (1994): 273–302.

Stephenson, Edward A. "The Beginnings of the Loss of Post-vocalic /r/ in North Carolina." *Journal of English Linguistics* 2 (1968): 57–77.

Thomas, Erik, and Guy Bailey. "The Origins of Monophthongal /ai/ in Southern Speech." Paper presented at SECOL 50, Memphis, Tenn., 1994.

Trudgill, Peter. *The Dialects of England*. Cambridge: Basil Blackwell, 1990.

———, ed. *Language in the British Isles*. Cambridge: Cambridge University Press, 1985.

Upton, Clive, David Parry, and J. D. A. Widdowson. *Survey of English Dialects: The Dictionary and Grammar*. London: Routledge, 1994.

Wolfram, Walt. "Reconsidering the Semantics of a- Prefixing. *American Speech* 63 (1988): 247–54.

Wolfram, Walt, and Donna Christian. *Appalachian Speech*. Arlington, Va.: Center for Applied Linguistics, 1976.

Wolfram, Walt, and Kevyn Creech. *Dialect and Harkers Island Speech: Dialects and the Ocracoke Brogue—an Eighth-Grade Curriculum*. Raleigh: North Carolina Language and Life Project, 1996.

Wolfram, Walt, and Natalie Schilling-Estes. "Moribund Dialects and the Endangerment Canon: The Case of the Ocracoke Brogue." *Language* 71.4 (1995): 696–721.

———. "On the Social Basis of Phonetic Resistance." In *Sociolinguistic Variation: Cata, Theory, and Analysis*, edited by Jennifer Arnold, Renée Blake, Brad Davidson, Scott Schwenter, and Julie Solomon, pp. 69–82. Stanford, Calif.: CSLI Publications, 1996.

Wolfram, Walt, Natalie Schilling-Estes, and Kirk Hazen. *Dialects and the Ocracoke Brogue: An Eighth-Grade Curriculum*. Raleigh: North Carolina Language and Life Project, 1995.

Wolfram, Walt, Natalie Schilling-Estes, Kirk Hazen, and Chris Craig. "The Sociolinguistic Complexity of Quasi-Isolated Southern Coastal Communities." In *Language Variation in the South Revisited*, edited by Cynthia Bernstein, Tom Nunnally, and Robin Sabino. Tuscaloosa: University of Alabama Press, 1996.

Wolfram, Walt, Natalie Schilling-Estes, Roscoe Johnson, James Peterson, and Yancey R. Hall. "Dialect Mixing and Ethnic Identity in Lumbee English." Paper presented at SECOL 50, Memphis, Tenn., 1994.

Index

O'Neal, Rex: performance phrase, 57; on meeting fieldworkers, 123–24; oyster story, 142

O'Neal Johnson, Joan: on brogue, 131

Ow sound: in language periods, 9, 59

Oy sound, 1, 15, 23, 50, 54, 56–58, 60, 106–7, 109, 111, 114, 121–24, 134–36

Ozark: resemblance to Ocracoke, 62, 64

Parsons, Elizabeth: on brogue, xvi

"Performance phrase," 50–51, 57, 59, 135. *See also* O'Neal, Rex

Plural *-s/-es* absence, 90–91, 111, 121

Positive *anymore*, 10, 20, 88, 98, 111–12

Pronoun *-n* ending, 91–92

Pronunciation, 50–73; *r*, 1, 18, 64–66, 72, 98, 106, 108; *oy*, 1, 54, 56–59, 106–7; *ow*, 1, 60; *ay*, 8, 54, 60, 105; *aw*, 18, 54; *h* retention, 23, 68–70, 109; British *t*, 54; *ah*, 57–58; *ar*, 59–60; *eh*, 61–63; *ih*, 61–63; syllable deletion, 67–68, 108; *-t* addition, 69, 72

Robeson County: resemblance to Ocracoke, 32, 102, 106. *See also* Lumbee Vernacular English

R sound, 1, 18, 64–66, 72, 98, 106, 108; saliency in North Carolina, 64; saliency in North, 65; *r*-lessness, 65, 66

Scarborough, Cathy: on pronunciation, 59

Scots-Irish: language influence of, 9, 10, 15, 27; migration of, 27; resemblance to Ocracoke, 77, 81, 87, 88

Shakespeare, William: language, 3, 5, 89; double negatives, 78; intensifiers, 89

Shakespearean English, as compared with Ocracoke English: similarities, 2; differences, 60. *See also* Britain: similarities to Ocracoke; Elizabethan English

Smith Island: resemblance to Ocracoke, 57, 78, 103, 106; *to* for *at*, 76

Spanish: double negatives, 93

Subject-verb agreement, 1, 10, 15, 81–82

Surnames, Ocracoke: Austin, 7; Ballance, 7; Bragg, 7; Gaskins, 7; Howard, 7; Jackson, 7; Midgett, 7; O'Neal, 7; Scarborough, 7; Stiron, 7; Williams, 7

Syllable deletion: initial, 67–68; medial, 67–68; final, 67–68, 108

-T addition, 69, 72

Tangier Island: resemblance to Ocracoke, 57, 78, 103, 106; *to* for *at*, 76

To for *at*, 75–76

Tourism: influence of, 52, 97, 120–21, 131, 134

Transportation, island, 120

Trudgill, Peter: on Ocracoke and England similarity, 53

Virginia Tidewater area: resemblance to Ocracoke, 7, 9, 103; *ow* sound, 69; *to* for *at*, 76

Vocabulary: examples of, 2, 28, 30, 31, 32, 33, 35, 36, 37, 38, 50, 52, 62, 70, 75, 84, 117, 121, 134; list of, 39–49; knowledge of, 100–103; quiz, 150–54

Weren't regularization, 11, 16, 23, 26, 28, 83–84, 114, 132

World War II, 20, 120–21; *r*-lessness, 66; *h* retention, 69; island transportation, 120

Y'all, 92–93